Speak Out Fearlessly

..and the world will listen to you

Yogesh Saini

First published in 2020 by

Becomeshakespeare.com

One Point Six Technologies Pvt Ltd.
119-123, 1st Floor, Building J2, B - Wing,
WadalaTruck Terminal, Wadala East, Mumbai,
Maharashtra, India, 400022.
T: +91 8080226699

ISBN - 978-93-90543-31-1

Disclaimer:

This is a work of creative non-fiction. Some names and identifying features have been changed or hidden to protect the identity of certain people and places.

The author in no way represents any company, corporation, famous figure, or brand, mentioned here in. The views expressed in this book are based on some wise and practical lessons learnt by the author in his life journey and are meant for motivational purpose only, not to replace a proper training or coaching or personal advice from an expert. Readers are advised to use discretion and proper guidance before using the techniques mentioned in the book.

Events, locales, and conversations have been recreated from the author's memories. Some work of fiction has been added to give a necessary flow, stuff and direction to the story. The information provided in the book does not claim to provide factual details of anyone or anything

Acknowledgments

I have to start by thanking my awesome wife, Mamta for all her patience and support. From reading early drafts to keeping the munchkins out of my hair so I could spend enough time undistracted. She was as important to this book getting done as I was. Thank you so much, dear.

I can't stop thanking my elder brother, Ajay, for keeping his unshakable support during my toughest times. You are the one I can always count on.

My mother, and late father, for their wonderful nurturing, and *sanskara*, which helped develop my mind in way that I look towards life positively.

Great regards and deep gratitude to the editor Arnaz Mehta, for all her kind patience and untiring support, without which completion of this book would have been a distant dream.

Thanks to everyone on the Scribe team who helped me so much. Special thanks to the ever-patient Publishing Manager, my amazing Scribe, and the greatest cover designer I could ever imagine.

A special thanks to my source of inspiration Mr. Akash Gautam, Mr Robin Sharma, and Mr. Arfeen Khan, whose motivation and directions gave me the right fuel to stay spirited and focused in my life.

Countless thanks to my beloved spiritual Guru Sri Sri Ravi Shankar for his blessings that always keep my spirit up and mind down-to-earth.

About the Author:

Yogesh Saini is a Communication Strategist and an English trainer. He is a founder of 'Speak Out Fearlessly' program through which he has interacted, inspired, and impacted more than 10,000 students and professionals. He's on a mission to help one million people become powerful communicators.

Ask yourself the following questions before you start reading:

1. Is each passing year of your life adding more tension, more frustration, more inactivity, increased illnesses, reducing your smiles every hour?

2. Do you have a dream?

3. Do you have the courage to be the architect of your own destiny?

Keep note of your honest answers

Take a pause… sit down and relax… close your eyes and see which way your current life is going.

Is it going the way you always wanted? Is it expanding? Is each passing year making you happier, making you fitter and leaving you more fulfilled?

The answer to these questions will open a window to the future. The answer will prove to be the key to tremendous possibilities in your future.

Once you have answered the above questions, here is another crucial question for you-

Do you believe your life will be inspirational?

Or, let me put it in another way:

Do you believe, that the way your present life is going, will one day transform you into an inspirational person?

If answer to this question is not a Confident 'YES,' it's time for you to wake up and look closely at your life.

So, it's the right time to

TAKE A PAUSE

SIT AND RELAX

CLOSE YOUR EYES FOR SOME MORE TIME

AND TAKE A FRESH LOOK AT

- HOW YOUR CURRENT LIFE IS GOING

- HOW THIS LIFE IS GOING TO SHAPE
  YOUR FUTURE!

When you do this, you'll realize that:

- ➢ your life should be better, because you *deserve* better.

- ➢ your life should be happier, because you *deserve* to be happier.

- ➢ you should be fitter, because you *don't deserve* illness and lethargy.

- ➢ you should be richer, because you *don't deserve* poverty.

- ➢ your life should be more fulfilling, because inner-fulfilment is the natural way of existence.

Let me humbly share with you a journey from mediocrity to finding a code of an ever-growing, expanding and fulfilling life. It's a story of a person, Kumar, how he orchestrated his destiny to fulfil his dream of becoming a powerful speaker.

Chapter 1

Moving Beyond the School That Failed Me

❖ **Trapped in Mediocrity**

Kumar was born in a small town in Haryana, India and his entire childhood was spent in his hometown. From the beginning, he was quite a sincere and calm guy. Having never seriously fought with anyone, he was well liked by all family members and neighbours.

His schooling was from a Hindi-medium Government-funded school; like most similar schools, his too was also run by people with the typical mentality. They would bother with everything but education. For discipline, students would be beaten to any degree; being scolded, or shouted at wasn't considered serious. The students were quite used to it. In fact, they would come back with a hidden smile if let off by the teacher only with scolding and no beating.

Discipline didn't include punctuality, something that even affected the teachers and principal. A 10-minute delay was a ritual which most teachers would follow, the principal included.

However, the school was a heaven for those students who didn't want to study and for those teachers who didn't want to teach. In the frequent absence of teachers, the unsupervised students could create a mess inside the classrooms; provided they kept the door closed, they could -and did – get away with it. Frequent holidays, on every and any small occasion, would ensure that students would never feel the importance of keeping track of their studies. The class toppers, Kumar among them, were entitled to immunity from punishments.

The school also had a Flagship Student Leadership Program, in which some chosen students, usually toppers, had to supervise the class when a teacher was absent, either on leaves or when not in mood to take the class and preferred to stay in the staff room. A message would usually be sent to the class monitor by a student messenger in such cases. The class monitor would write down the names of the miscreants on the board, and thus held a great authority as he used to be the one to decide which students were to be beaten up by the teacher. The fate of many students depended upon his discretion. Many a time, the toppers would ask the questions to their fellow students, check their notebooks, and, at times, even exams. This would also train the students management skills from a very early stage. Students became independent as the teaching was a formality. Thus, the overall quality of his entire schooling was ludicrous, nothing more than a procedure.

Though he was hard working and sincere, the poor schooling failed to add an enriching experience in his life and left him poor in skills and personality. His hard work had paid off in examination marks; but like the others of his class, he also lacked many essential life skills, especially communication.

Unfortunately, he was not the only victim to a disoriented schooling. But his entire friend circle, namely Brahmjeet, Naveen, Dinesh, Virender, Pankaj, Satyendra, etc., who all were from the same school, were negatively impacted. They were all commendable students who had great potential and possible bright futures, if not for the schooling hampering their early learning.

For a plant to grow healthy, it requires two important things. Firstly, the right soil, and secondly, the right caretaker to help nurture and protect. These students were among those unfortunate plants, who were planted in the wrong soil – gotten into the wrong school – and their caretakers – teachers - were not dutiful. Too young and innocent at that time, none of them realized the insidious damage they had been subjected to. They merely enjoyed their school days thoroughly.

Kumar suffered from this very badly. The reflection of this educational backwardness wrongly shaped his mindset and ruined his confidence. It left him feeling diffident in front of others; in college, he found himself lacking. Even after completing the college, he found himself incompetent. This constant inferiority complex gripped him so hard that he failed to unshackle himself. This ultimately ceased all further opportunities from reaching him.

He'd had dreams when he was in college. He was

sincere and hardworking. He made some attempts to open himself up, like performing in a group dance onstage, conducting some lectures etc. These successful attempts had some positive impact on him. His confidence increased to some extent.

Nonetheless, he had random dreams or fantasies – like many youngsters – his included influencing people through by giving speeches from the stage, starting a chain of excellent schools, visiting the seven wonders of the world, all the adventurous activities like sky-diving, bungee jumping etc. His dreams would sometimes excite him too. When it came to taking steps to chase them, his inferiority complex would diffuse all excitement and tie him down.

This pattern would repeat whenever he thought of reaching for something during college, whether performing on stage in a cultural event or facing interviews.

Over time, every big challenge appeared daunting and he started finding excuses to get out of them, something which carried on to his normal life too.

"The tendency to save yourself from your inner fears and challenges takes you closer to them."

Like every bad habit, this one too aided him in the beginning but in the long run, it showed how harmful it could be; procrastination, distraction, and loss of enthusiasm started becoming normal without him realizing it.

Slowly, he turned into a person who neither had enough confidence nor the right skills to face challenges; which resulted in him believing that his dreams were all distant fancies, that he would never be able to achieve them unless some miracle intervened. So, instead of working towards improving, he chose mediocrity.

He accepted his mediocrity as the only real possibility.

As a result outside daydreaming, a meaningful and expanding life slipped beyond his reach.

Chapter 2
Failing Three Interviews

❖ Interviews –My Biggest Fear

"Where is Kumar?" Brahmjeet asked Kumar's mother. Kumar and Brahmjeet have been childhood friends and know each other inside out.

"He's gone out, probably to the park."

"Ok. In that case, I know where he'll be," Brahmjeet, knowing exactly where to find him, went to look.

Kumar sat on a grassy slope in the park near his home. He usually went to this beautiful park for occasional exercise, gossip and to kill time with friends. It was a moonless night in early winter. As it was dark already, not a lot of people were around. That was why he had come to spend time alone. The grass was a little damp because of the early fog. Had it been a normal day, he would have loved watching the carpet of moisture on the grass, reflecting the park lights. Anybody walking would get the impression of walking over starry skies.

But this day was different. He was in a different mood. His life wasn't going the way he'd always wanted. His shortcomings, fearful mind, habit of making excuses, it had all taken a toll on his progress and hopes. What happened today, had simply salted his injury. Now, the frustration peaked and felt unbearable, there was no way he could get out of this unsuccessful phase.

He'd failed an interview that day. This may appear trivial, but it was his third in succession, and it had shaken him badly. It hadn't felt *that* bad, when he failed his first interview.

On the day of his first interview, he'd been too nervous to enter the cabin; he couldn't even say good morning confidently. The interviewer was a middle-aged man with a French beard, his intense gaze, hard to bear. It was took him tremendous effort to maintain eye contact.

He suddenly felt his blank mind, when asked to introduce himself. He swallowed with difficulty before speaking. However, the interviewer was kind, and humbly asked him to leave the room after 4 or 5 minutes, and preserved his dignity.

When he came out, he thought of an excuse to give his friends and family. He said the interviewer asked some out of bound questions. Everyone easily accepted this. It being his first interview, he justified every negative thing as normal to himself. He successfully hid the fact that he was neither skilled nor prepared for the interview. But this successful hiding was the first step on the wrong path.

When he failed the second interview, he pretended again, this time he said he'd performed well but as only limited vacancies were available, he didn't make the cut. He was relieved that he managed to successfully cover the ugly truth. The truth that he had wasted so much of his time that he never actually worked hard enough to gain the necessary skills and confidence. He'd failed the two interviews now.

Sitting by himself that day, gave him some time to reflect on what all was happening in his life. He realized that he'd wasted most of his time dreaming about a good life – chatting with friends was his favourite pastime, the topics would vary, loopholes in the current education system, politics, international relations among many others. He was good at discussion and he would often give arguments in support of his point of view which were hard to counter. He loved such discussions, partially to have a sense of victory which was otherwise missing in his practical life, something that he felt only when he won their discussions.

He found it more convenient to hide the ugly truth, than face it. Slowly, these lies grew and kept growing smothering any possibility for growth.

There are times the Universe shakes us, jolts us, and pushes us by sending us some setback. It's the Universe's way of making us face reality, maybe that's why this third failure shook him badly. People had always thought of him as a sincere, intelligent, and hard-working person. Failing multiple interviews was a stain on that image. He found it very hard to face this immutable fact, and even harder to let this news get around.

"What are you doing here at this time? What happened at your interview?" Brahmjeet asked him curiously, though he had realized that there was no good news.

"Nothing. Another failure." He said with a heavy voice without looking up. He hadn't even reacted to Brahmjeet's sudden presence.

"What happened? I've never seen you this worried!" Brahmjeet exclaimed in concern.

"Yes. You know I've always hidden my failures from people, and even from myself. I've always made excuses to make my failures sound reasonable." He replied honestly and continued, "I've achieved nothing in life. I've spoiled my life. I've wasted all my potential by simply killing time." Kumar buried his head in his folder arms atop his knees in melancholy and stopped talking.

Brahmjeet sighed deeply and said nothing for some time. Kumar stayed in that posture for quite some time, not expecting his friend to console him.

After a long silence, Brahmjeet spoke up. "There's no point in talking about the interview when you're already so depressed. The only thing I want to tell you is a story, a true story. Will you listen?"

"I'm not in a mood to listen. But, since you asked, it won't be pointless. Go ahead," Kumar sighed, knowing that his sensible friend was not so immature as to try to entertain him at this moment to make him feel better.

"There was a girl who was a national level volleyball player in India. She was traveling by train in 2011 when a bunch of robbers suddenly attacked the co-passengers. Everyone complied and meekly followed their instructions. But this girl had guts, she resisted. It seemed she was the only man among the so called men on that train. But she paid a price. She was pushed and thrown out of the running train. She landed on the parallel tracks with one leg over the track. To her horror, another train passed and ran over her leg. She spent the whole night in between the tracks in excruciating pain, horror and helplessness." Brahmjeet paused for a moment looking at his grave expression.

"Uff…." Kumar's sharp wince conveyed his empathy for her plight.

Brahmjeet looked at him and went on, "The next day, some villagers spotted her and took her to a hospital. But it was like a series of misfortunate events. The doctors told her that her leg had to be amputated immediately. She was completely alone and forced to decide, with no friends and no relatives around; it was extremely tough for her to make this decision. But she had guts and agreed to the surgery. Preparations for the operation were about to begin when she was informed that the hospital had run out of anaesthesia. However the operation was urgent."

"Oh my god!" Kumar couldn't say more due to shock.

"She was a true hero. She allowed the doctors to perform the operation while she was awake. The operation went ahead and the leg was amputated," Brahmjeet paused again, looked at Kumar and continued telling the story after finding him totally absorbed.

"Imagine the shock of losing your leg when you are a 23-year-old national level volleyball player with a bright career ahead of you. Anyone would have shattered. For many, this would've been the end of a bright phase of life and the beginnings of a victim's story, which would continue for rest of their life. But as I said she had guts. For her, this tragedy marked the beginning of another brighter phase of life." The emphatic words shone through his bright eyes.

"She was inspired by cricketer Yuvraj Singh who had successfully overcome cancer as well as Bachendri Pal, the first Indian woman to climb Mount Everest that same year. So, now she too decided to pursue her dreams, no matter what happened."

"Sounds impressive. But what was her dream?" Kumar interrupted.

"Did you know in 2013, she became the World's first

female amputee to climb Mount Everest? Since then, she's climbed all the highest peaks in the world."

"Incredible!" This was all Kumar could respond.

"Her book *Born Again on The Mountain* was later launched by PM Modi. She was also awarded Padma Shri." Brahmjeet's voice gained some gravity at this point.

"Indeed. She deserves it." Kumar agreed absolutely. "But what's her name?"

"Arunima Sinha. Remember her story when you need motivation." His words were so profound that they reverberated in Kumar's mind for a long time.

By the time the story finished, Kumar was restless as something prodded his heart, though, no sign of change was externally visible. He went back home and googled Arunima Sinha; the more he read about her, the more restless he became.

Chapter 3

The Powerful Story Breaks the Inertia

❖   **Some stories are transformational**

After a day or two while on a calm morning walk, he had an idea that transformed the way he looked at himself and forced him to introspect.

Despite being a hard-working, sincere, and spiritual person, he was only leading a mediocre life. He'd had big dreams in life, but had never tried to chase them. Like everyone, he had always believed that he was not born to live and die in a mediocre life like an ordinary person. He had a firm belief that if he took steps, he could easily change the course of his life, yet he never took them. He never took a step towards achieving his dream.

This was the first time he was shaken.

He thought, "I always justified my inaction and procrastination. I always said that I was happy. Happiness is all one needs in life, so it was enough for me."

He wrote down this realization in a notebook, "Nothing could be more damaging than making excuses for not following your dreams. Such justifications killed all my possibilities and left me passively satisfied. A person who was satisfied but stunted. Hollow happiness had become my excuse for inaction."

He recalled everything about his past.

"In no time, my wasted days erased my precious months and golden years from my life. It all happened

right before my eyes but I couldn't realize it. I'm now left with abysmal poverty where I lack everything." He sadly concluded.

He made notes on what he called 'symptoms' of such attitude arising from this kind of poverty. He had following ones:

- *Lack of confidence* –because he had never dared in life.

- *Lack of important skills*–because he had never learnt, refined, or worked on his skills

- *Lack of a great social circle* –because he had only few contacts and always surrounded by mediocre people; his social network remained poor.

- *Lack of rich experience* –As he hadn't learnt much in his life, he didn't have much valuable experience to share with his loved ones and no beautiful memories to cherish. As time goes by, one feels that desperate lack.

These symptoms were indicative of a palpable frustration brewing within him.

Unfortunately, he couldn't do much about it as he felt he was too late. He was apprehensive that eventually, this mediocrity would become his normal, his reality.

He told himself "What Arunima Sinha achieved after losing her leg, people usually can't when they *have* legs. It's about chasing your dreams or staying in place, staying mediocre."

A little more motivated and enthusiastic, he continued writing in his notebook.

Facts the powerful story of Arunima Sinha re-establishes:

❖ SELF-CONFIDENCE IS THE ONLY KEY TO A GRAND LIFE:

She could have easily lived a life of a victim. Most people would chose to live as victims after such a tragedy.

He remembered his college friend who squandered the golden years of his life after a break-up, lost into the gloom of drink, inactivity, and depression. He lost all confidence and enthusiasm for life and consequently blocked all chances for progress in his future too.

A painful tragedy comes uninvited in different forms like a loved one's death, a break-up or divorce, losing your job, a business loss, a sudden health hazard etc., but it's always your choice to stay in pain or not. You can stay in a depressed state for months, years or quickly and confidently come out of it, to be a hero of your own life, like Arunima Sinha.

'Our life is more about our choices and less about what happens to us' he tells himself.

❖ YOUR CONFIDENCE IS ALWAYS INSIDE YOU:

A tragedy can give you a serious wound–like shock or amputation–but **No tragedy can take your confidence away unless you allow it**. Even when you think it's disappeared, it's inside, hidden behind your doubts. Your confidence awaits silently to be unveiled.

Arunima Sinha's experience shows that confidence is always inside you.

One event flashed to his mind.

****

Once during his college years, his friend Lalit and he were asked to perform a group dance on stage by the college authority for College Pharmacy week. Forget dancing before an audience of 300 people, Kumar had never been onstage before! This news sent a shiver down his spine. It was a massive task. "How will I dance onstage? How can I practice in a short time of 5 days?" Questions started running through his mind. A great fear overtook him, leaving him confused and unable to move.

Struggling with this fear, he unconsciously headed towards an office in the college. This was the cabin of the senior-most faculty of his college, professor Dr. J.D. Sharma. Everyone in the college respected him. He was a short, septuagenarian professor, an honorary teacher of anatomy and physiology, whose persona, knowledge, and skills were unmatched.

Kumar expressed his frustration and fear to the professor, who smiled after listening and asked him to sit down. "Are you angry at the college authority for giving you such a task on short notice, or are you angry with yourself because of your fear?"

This unexpected question was extremely embarrassing. He spoke after a long pause.

"Honestly speaking, I'm angry at myself sir. I'm angry because I feel too afraid to perform onstage. Anger at the College Authority is just a way of hiding my fear." He looked down in shame.

There was a palpable silence in the cabin.

When Kumar looked up and found the professor smiling at him.

"Please, guide me sir"

"Are you sure?"

"Yes sir, I'll do as you say"

"You are not in a state to make a commitment my dear. A mind in confusion can't follow through on its

commitment. You should come back, after an hour. Right now, you should go and clear your mind."

Kumar knew that the professor was right. So, he followed his advice. Before he could leave though, the professor asked him "Kumar, just ask yourself the following questions-

- *Do you want to overcome this fear that is crippling you?*

- *Do you think that the confidence you are going to gain after giving the performance outweighs all the risks?*

Just return with the answers to these questions," the professor smiled again, turned around and went back to his work.

He spent an hour on the terrace. He was alone, mulling over the professor's questions. He knew the answers but his doubtful mind was not ready at first to accept the answers. The hour gave him a clarity.

When he went back to the professor he said, "Sir, I have the answers. Thank you so much."

"All the best, my dear. God bless you." Kumar left the room after reverently touching his wise teacher's feet.

He started vigorous practice for the dance competition with his friend. He was enthusiastic about his first dance performance on stage. Things started going his way after he became determined

The first big hurdle was the strict class timetable, which he could not skip. Nevertheless, the next day began with good news that the class schedule had been relaxed for the participants; allowing them to skip their classes and focus on their performance. The second piece of news came in the afternoon, the director had permitted the participants to stay back until 9 pm. It was almost next to impossible since he was usually averse to cultural programs and obsessed with academics. Now they had plenty of time to practice, from 9 am to 9 pm.

The day after that, everyone's costumes arrived for the dress rehearsal. Getting costumes were usually a huge headache as they would often arrive late, sometimes too late; a fact every participant dreaded.

The day of their performance was cool, pleasant. Both friends were confident and busy giving final touches, getting some last-minute feedback from their friends, Silky, Rishu, Upasna, and Sandeep who were helping them out with feedback and opinions on the practice.

Unexpectedly, they got cold feet minutes before the performance while waiting for their turn. Both looked at each other apprehensively though they didn't talk about it. They quietly acknowledged the fact that this anxiety wasn't easy to bear. Every passing second had their heart beating faster.

Kumar closed his eyes for a moment. The words of his teacher came to his mind, "The advantages of this performance outweigh the disadvantages."

A smile appeared on his face and he looked at Lalit confidently. Like fear, confidence is also contagious and his smile brought one on Lalit's face as well.

Finally, came the announcement of their names. They both looked at each other, gave each other a confident hug and fist-bump and moved towards the stage. The rest, as they say is history.

Their performance was awarded 'Best Group Dance' at the time of prize distribution.

With this victory, the dam was broken. All unnecessary thoughts and fears evaporated like smoke. Since then both, performed innumerable times on stage. In fact, they fell in love with stage performance that day.

****

He smiled, remembering the event after a long time. It infused some thrill in his heart.

❖ ONCE YOU BELIEVE IT, YOU ACHIEVE IT:

The whole story has the theme 'believe in your dreams' because **'Believing is achieving'** or **'You achieve only that which you believe."**

Arunima Sinha had no doubt about her dreams. She knew that she had to pursue her dream of climbing Everest even with a prosthetic leg.

"The process of goal chasing can't be on and off. However, the power of belief determines your regularity."- He added this to his notebook. Her story sparked the thrill of achievement in him. Now, it inspired him to pursue his dreams.

Chapter 4

Discovering The Key To Success In Interviews

❖ **Realization of Power of Conversation**

It took Kumar many failed interviews and a few years to understand, analyse and decode the entire process of interviews. For him, any news of an interview was an instant electric shock. He was like a small kid, who is afraid of injections and tries his best to avoid them. He too, always first thought of evading the interview in his mind. But he had to force himself to do it, to get it over with. This fierce tussle of going or not-going for the interview would always occur. It would suck out all his enthusiasm, leaving him drained and exhausted. What possibility for victory can one estimate for an exhausted soldier going into battle? None.

This was the reason all his interviews were total chaos.

First, he'd get exhausted overthinking about the interview result. Then, this exhaustion would prevent him from mustering all his strength. A scared and exhausted mind can only focus on the negative aspects. Consequently, his body language, facial expressions and tone would also be severely impacted, which further reduced his overall effectiveness. Lastly, due to his cluttered subconscious mind, he couldn't focus on what to say, how to present himself, and what kind of outcome of the interview he wanted.

However, gradually things were changing as he was slowly learning the art of facing an interview.

Realization of the Power of conversation:

Once, Kumar was travelling by bus. Due to his exhaustion he didn't realize that he had dozed off. A sudden thud, followed by a heavy jolt, snapped him awake. Then several shrieks and loud commotion around snapped him to complete alertness. He couldn't make out what was happening, but courtesy his natural reflexes, he found himself pressing his hands against the back of seat in front of him. There was a long scraping sound around the front and the bus dangerously tilted towards the driver side. Apparently, something had gone wrong with the front right side. When the bus stopped after a few seconds, he came to know that the tire had come loose.

Everyone was scared and panicked. The driver was also horrified, and had felt the maximum impact since he sat right above the affected tire. Children started crying loudly. When Kumar looked towards the front, he saw the conductor rising from his seat and speaking loudly in the local dialect, "It's a common thing my brothers, sometimes it happens, don't worry. You will all safely reach your destination on time."

He saw the immediate impact of his words. His words were a powerful medicine to the panicky souls on the bus, Kumar among them.

Soon, everyone was out of the bus, and in another 15 minutes the passengers were adjusted on the other bus.

At home, while writing his journal he recalled this incident and thought "If I could feel relief after listening to the conductor, how effective words can be in any situation."

His second thought was to pen down and analyse the words: **"It's a common thing, so no need to worry. You all will reach your destination on time."**

His eyes glinted when he went over the words of this semi-educated bus conductor, words which made him a true leader in his eyes.

He summarized the event in the following way:

1. First, the bus conductor wasted no time in dispelling people's fear by saying that it's a common problem.

   However, he wasn't stating facts. In fact, this was the only time when I've come across this type of problem. I'm sure that it was not a common situation. But by saying that it was, he successfully gave the impression to the passengers that they weren't in danger. He also assured everyone that the situation would be handled easily. He calmed the building panic through his words. It's a psychology trick, that when a situation is presented as a common one, it no longer causes dread and people deal with it more capably. Exactly what he did with his words.

2. Secondly, he assured everyone that they would reach their destination on time. This further strengthened the truth of his previous statement— the situation wasn't serious. This relieved people and they could deal with the situation without panicking. So, while what he said may not be factual, but it was absolutely required.

   This also means the most challenging or unexpected situation can be made to appear manageable with a change in perception.

This clarity led to a significant development in Kumar's life. His biggest issue was 'facing interviews'. He dreaded them. Over time, he realized the same method could be used to deal with other issues of life as well, like an interview.

This simple analysis of the bus incident, motivated him to experiment with his life. If he was right, this method would solve the biggest issue of his life-Interviews.

First, he simplified the problem. His biggest problem was facing an interview. So, he penned down all his thoughts that he usually had before an interview. He also considered when his next interview was scheduled so that he could observe his thoughts better. He realized that:

1. **Almost all his thoughts about the interview were negative.**

He divided them into two categories:

a) **Panicked**: These thoughts were all about his weaknesses and fear of being exposed by the interviewer. For example, most of the thoughts were like

- what if the interviewer finds mistakes in my English?

- what if he asks questions about subjects in graduation in which he was weak?

- what if he asks about my plans or my strengths and weaknesses, which he was not clear about?

b) **Escapist**: Most of his thoughts were about how to dodge the blow of the interview. He would think up various weird ideas:

- He thought of falling seriously sick so that he could miss it

- Other times he would imagine the interviewer falling sick and the interview being rescheduled.

- Sometimes, he would come up with a tragedy or a natural calamity to delay the interview.

He realized that most of the solutions offered by his mind were to avoid the situation.

2. **Majorly the thoughts were repetitive.**

These thoughts always started 2-3 days before the interview. Each time he remembered the pending interview, these kinds of thoughts would fill his mind. If he remembered it 10 times during the day, every time he would have the same repetitive negative thoughts.

Interestingly, he also observed that similar thoughts would repeat every time he scheduled an interview. He studied this observation carefully. Essentially every time he thought of an interview, his mind went over the same thoughts, and then it would try to avoid the day by imagining some weird and unrealistic solutions.

This newfound clarity about his own mind shocked him but he didn't have trouble accepting all this. It was quite fascinating for him to see how all this was revealed by simply writing down observations. He could also feel the extraordinary power of observation.

"Observation is a magical teacher and a best informer. It reveals something potentially life-changing about yourself that you never knew."

Now, he had three extremely precious revelations:

a) All these fears were products of his own mind. His mind had given fear a significant space to occupy. As a result, he had a fear filled mind.

b) Consequently, there was no space left for positive thoughts. The clouds of negative thoughts shrouded all positive possibilities. Each time he faced an interview, he didn't have any positive thoughts.

c) Escapism is not a solution. Interviews are the essential part of any selection process. No professional can or should try to bypass them. So, the only real solution lay in facing, not evading them. Preparing with a positive mindset is the only solution.

Now the issue was no longer dreadful. This meant the unnecessary fear about the problem was gone and he realized that the real issue wasn't the fear but the lack of a solution.

This simplified the whole issue completely. Now the focus was to prepare and not to think.

That evening he was sitting in his study. The right wall was filled with book shelves until a reachable height, which he would call his personal library and was very proud of. However, this pride was unfounded, most of the books were those he had purchased, but never read beyond a few pages.

Maintaining the library was one of his favourite pastimes. A cursory glance over the collection of books ranging from science fiction to whodunit to spirituality, would always infuse his mind with an impression of opulence. This was the only richness in his otherwise ordinary existence.

Sitting in his desk chair he again thought of the bus incident.

Remembering the bus conductor's words further put him at ease, "It's a common thing. Nothing serious about it."- this gave him a required thrust to uplift his sinking mind. Now all he had to do was to simplify his responses to all those baffling questions, which usually scared him. Now he knew how to deal with those questions:

-What if the interviewer comes to know about my poor English?

I will humbly acknowledge it as a weakness. I may also add the effort put in to improve this essential skill.

-What if he asks questions about subjects in graduation in which he was weak?

I would simply state that I don't remember everything that I've studied. I will also show that I'm confident about the subject of my interest.

-What if he asks about my plans?

I will say that I've yet to figure out as I was not clear until graduating. But I'm working passionately in my area of interest and the same can be said about my life journey.

These thoughts brought immense clarity and a huge relief. A satisfied smile and a spark in his eyes were proof of a new hope in his life. Now he was confident about handling these kinds of questions.

He concluded, **"The interviewer doesn't' expect a perfect answer, all he wants is a clear, precise, and confident answer."**

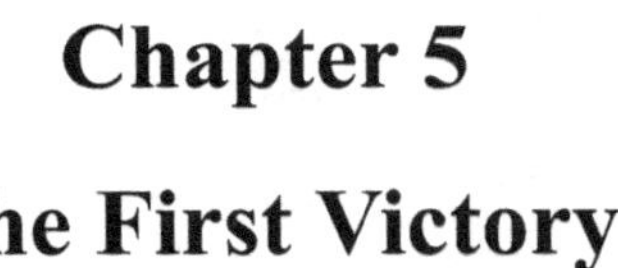

Chapter 5

The First Victory

❖ **The First Successful Interview**

He'd applied for the post of a sales executive for a major pharmaceutical company in Chandigarh. Soon, the much-awaited call for an interview came. This time he was more alert.

As per his usual tendency, the first reaction was obviously negative. Reading the interview email sent instant shivers down through his spine, increased his heart rate, and a plethora of negative thoughts began running circles around his mind.

He had prepared his mind for this. It was time to implement the new pattern- simplifying the problem. He told himself, "Everything is fine, it's not a big issue, so no need to worry. Let's focus on preparing."

It instantaneously quieted most thoughts, unburdened his mind, and calmed him. Almost instantly, his heart rate was back to normal, and his mind focused.

The next step was planning and execution. This clear and positive state of mind was a new experience. It was the first time he was at ease, after scheduling an interview.

For the first time, the chain of negative thoughts was broken. He held the key to stay balanced in a face of a challenge. This felt magical, unbelievable. He could feel a transformation. It was a significant step forward in attaining an unfazed confidence and laser beam focus, which he had read frequently about in spiritual books.

He knew what the next step was- preparing for the interview 3 days away.

He made a list of his weak and strong areas.

- He emphasized on overall body language, tone and presentation skill, rather than a fluent English, which he didn't' have.

He decided to work on his introduction.

- For this he recorded his practices. Within three days, he made over 20 videos, analysed them, and improvised every time with a specific aspect he noticed.

Next were the problematic questions.

- A list of all potential and probable questions along with their answers. He called his experienced friends for feedback. Then he practiced several times again keeping his focus on high confidence and precise answers by removing superfluous words from his answers.

- He also did mock interviews in a room set up like the real thing to work on body language, posture, eye contact, etc. and it helped develop an overall effective presentation.

This way of preparing was novel and exciting. Each practice increased his confidence.

"This was like playing cricket," he thought for a moment, "There too you do all of this. You're aware of your strengths and weaknesses. You manage with what you have rather than think about what you don't. You anticipate possible attacks from opponents and prepare yourself accordingly. Then, you play the game with enthusiasm and vigour, unbothered by the possibility of defeat."

The fear of failing an interview had long been replaced with newfound interest in preparing; keeping negative thoughts at bay which would have hampered him otherwise.

The morning of the interview, he was filled with both excitement and apprehension. Although he was confident in his preparation, the old tendency of clinging to negativity wouldn't die overnight. For the duration of the 6-hour journey to Chandigarh, he oscillated between excitement and nervousness.

This interview was a test of his newfound confidence, his novel preparation method, and his magical key. A lot was at stake, not just the job.

He entered the interview room and was greeted by a man in early 40s, with short hair and moderate moustache. This disciplined looking man asked him to sit giving the impression of one who wants to listen to only what is important, nothing extra.

The interviewer looked askance at him. "Why are you not wearing a tie?" Though Kumar wore a suit, he hadn't bothered with a tie since no one usually did. Now it would be a reference point for the future.

This first unusual question came out as a bolt from the blue. It was curve ball right at the beginning, not ideal for someone like him who already struggled with interviews. But obviously he couldn't complain to the interviewer about it. However, simplification had become his mantra and instead of getting perplexed, he maintained his composure by giving a simple reply with a pleasant smile.

"Sir, actually I received an email for this interview on Friday, when I was out of town. I didn't get time to buy one. I called the company headquarters Friday evening to postpone the interview by one day to shop accordingly, but they said it wasn't possibility. That was why I came for the interview like this. My mistake sir, apologies. But I recognize very well how important it is for any professional in sales and marketing to present a good first impression."

The interviewer nodded; Kumar could clearly see that his apology and the last sentence were master strokes.

He observed a subtle change in his expressions. The interviewer was looking less threatening now, because either he had softened or Kumar was more confident, whatever the case, he was more at ease now.

"Please introduce yourself."

This was something he knew he could do easily; he responded in a little higher than a normal tone. He emphasized his ability to recognize weaknesses and his commitment to working on them, which he supported with some real life examples.

"Who is the role model in your life." The next question was fired quickly and he was glad that he had prepared. He explained feeling more confident, using greater fluency, careful not to sound as if he had crammed the answers.

"There are 12 more candidates waiting outside for their turn. In a minute, prove that you are better than them." The interviewer had a smirk when asking this question. He leaned back in the chair and crossed arms behind his head, confident this question would trip him up.

"Sorry sir, but I disagree. I believe it would be foolish to compare myself with others. Instead I can only assure you that under the guidance of my seniors, you will see my performance chart showing an upward trend in growth each month and year. That's all I can say."

He wrapped up his answer with longer than necessary eye contact. He'd built up his confidence throughout the interview and was curiously checking the interviewer's reactions. His smile told Kumar that he'd done a good job in this short interview.

Later, he couldn't believe the convincing answers he'd given. He kept smiling and left the premises without a care for the result of the interview.

When he wrote about his experience in his notebook, his way of writing had also changed. It had become precise and compelling. He wrote the important points:

> **The interviewer sits there to select, not to reject.** So, be calm and think that they're there only to select you.

> **Success depends on you, not the interviewer.** You must convince yourself first, before convincing the interviewer.

> **You don't achieve victory on the day of the interview, but earlier in your mind.** Your preparation with right mindset helps you gain victory long before the interview itself. The interview is a mere reflection of your preparation along with your mindset.

The next day, Kumar received an email for the last round of the interview. It was scheduled 2 days later. The first thing he did was to buy a good tie for his interview suit and left for the next round.

This round was a formality. It focused on checking original documents, signing papers, informative sessions about the company, the work culture, and the reporting managers etc. He was out of the premises within 2 hours. His soaring confidence showed in the wide smile throughout the rest of the day.

Chapter 6

A New Milestone

❖ Interview for a B-school

Beyond the success at the interview, it showed that the first time he practiced with dedication and won. Essentially, he had orchestrated this win with the correct planning and execution. The joy of getting a job was secondary.

It was the beginning of a new journey for someone who'd gained clarity about his strengths, his actions and more importantly the direction of his life.

He attended the next two interviews just to check his own level and the veracity of his newfound method. He also wanted to test his improvement in the quality of interaction. Dismally, he realized that in the field of Sales and marketing almost all interviews are conducted in a similar fashion giving the same kind of experience. It also reflected how comfortable he had become with the interview process, at least in his field.

After realizing that every type of interview is different with its own challenges, Kumar noticed that the repetitive facing of interviews left a distasteful cliched feeling.

He ran into an old school friend while hanging out in the market in Chandigarh one day. His friend told him that he was preparing for CAT, Common Admission Test for premier B-schools in India. This was the first time he had heard of any such entrance test. His friend also extolled the glory of some of India's finest B-schools and how one's life could transform if they could make it to them.

The discussion was long and Kumar found it quite intriguing. He was already looking for something exciting and promising for his own professional life. He had some vague dreams for himself but had no clear idea about how to achieve them. This new path looked right and clear. But how to travel it, was still unclear.

He discussed in detail about how he was preparing for this entrance, eligibility, and stuff. In excitement, the same day he visited one of the best coaching centres in the city, as recommended by his friend, and took all the necessary details. He also met a faculty member for more understanding about this new professional journey. The elaborate discussion gave him an improved understanding of the entrance test and the MBA as a course and his own suitability for all this.

He left the centre thrilled. He got a new ambition, to get admission in a premier B-school in India. He decided to attempt the entrance test and accordingly started preparations 7-8 months in advance. He knew that to get admission, it was necessary to pass extremely challenging rounds of Group Discussions and Personal Interviews conducted by different institutions after the written exam. But his undaunted spirit pushed him to take on this challenge.

He started his preparation enthusiastically. He got a fantastic friend circle in which everyone was equally zealous about MBA.

In their batch of 18 students, they were 6 friends who were close. Kumar and his entire group of friends Gargi, Parmjeet, Nitin, Sonam and Harman had a very strong bond with each other. Each passing month strengthened the bond between them. Their group was famous at the academy; known for being extremely active, sincere, and fun loving.

Even their teachers would appreciate them. When they would sit for studying, hours passed in complete silence. If you eavesdropped, you could hardly figure out that a group of people were inside. It remained an unsolved puzzle for other students that how the whole group got up from their seats at exactly same time for lunch break even if they sat in different rooms.

They also had a remarkably similar intelligence and behaviour. They were also famous for the mess they create while partying; but being kind towards the office boy, they would leave no trace of any muck before leaving the party classroom except the smell.

During lunch or snack breaks, everybody in the coaching centre knew this group would be sitting on a raised platform under a banyan tree across from the centre a few yards away from an always busy tea-stall.

Because of their loud discussions, passers-by would easily make out that these guys were practicing spoken English or some group-discussion.

Sonam was the least talkative and most soft-spoken among them, while Harman was an impressive speaker but the naughtiest one, Parmjeet and Gargi were most sincere and regular but had poor English, Nitin was the most irregular one but had very sound judgement, calculative mind, and was always helpful. Overall, this was a group where they would complement each other, not compete. People would call them an ideal group of friends.

After preparing for months, most of them from the group were able to crack the test except Harman and Nitin. They decided to go for some alternative tests, which they successfully did.

After clearing CAT, they changed their preparation from theory to group discussion and Interviews. The passion and regularity remained the same, only content had changed. Now the discussions were not restricted to any confined places like classroom or GD-Hall, but everywhere. It would get louder and fiercer near the tea-stall. The stairs at Sukhna lake was their favourite place where they would sit for hours preparing for their contents and discussing on various topics.

Now after a month or so, everyone started waiting for their GD/PI calls from their respective B-schools.

A Tale of Two Weird Interviews:

Kumar and his friend Gargi were invited for the next round-a Group Discussion and Interview-with a premier MBA institute.

On the day, Kumar was apprehensive; he'd prepared for the interviews but it wasn't the normal type he was now used to. This interview was for a premier MBA institute and he was competing with the best in India. Another thing that bothered him was that it was for the MBA (International Business) course, an alien field for him as nobody in his far extended family had done any business. The only ludicrous reason he had chosen this field was that he found the title MBA (IB) appealing, and liked the college and its infrastructure.

Gargi on the other hand, had a business background and acumen. Her only challenge was English. She'd managed to qualify the written test, but GD/PI was going to be a big hurdle.

On the day, both were nervous for different reasons. Kumar, due to his lack of knowledge about the chosen field and Gargi due to her poor spoken English. They knew each other's strengths but in such situations your mind clings to the negative.

On the way to the interview venue, both discussed

their problems. That's when he remembered the bus conductor and the rule of simplifying the problem.

"I've got something that might work." murmured Kumar dubiously.

Gargi wondered what he was up to. She believed that nothing would work in such a short time against this insurmountable problem.

"Silly psychological tactics won't work," she retorted, "But right now I'm willing to try anything."

Kumar said, "We will make our introduction very special"

"What do you mean?"

"Let's start with our name followed by our strengths."

"How will that help? I don't understand."

"Give me two minutes and I'll show you." Kumar wrote something down and after some editing, he was happy with it. He showed it to Gargi.

"Sir, I'm Kumar and I'm a great believer of ancient Indian scriptures. My favourite is the Shrimad Bhagwat Gita whose teachings have totally transformed me. Its reading has brought me unbridled confidence and immense courage to sacrifice anything for my purpose. I found it to be enlightening and if understood correctly, it can make anyone a creator of their destiny." This left Gargi impressed and in awe.

"What makes you so sure about this? I mean, the introduction sounds good, but do you honestly think it will help?" Fear naturally doesn't disappear easily and the same was true here.

"See the way I see it; the interviewer is interested in finding a person who clearly knows their strength. He may choose to ignore weaknesses if he sees that we know our strengths. I know my strength lies in my voracious reading and understanding of Indian scriptures. I also know that my choosing a field in which I know nothing is my biggest weakness."

"You're assuming the interviewer is naïve to be easily outwitted with such a trick? I seriously doubt this illogical idea." Gargi was unconvinced, but Kumar forged on.

"We're not trying to fool the interviewer, we're trying to show our strengths in a way that he isn't interested in our weaknesses. I think we're selected based on strengths and rejected over weaknesses. It's up to us to highlight what we choose. My gut says this simple tweaking with our introduction will succeed."

A brief silence followed.

"Remember what our teacher Mr. Akash Gautam once

said-maintain control of an interview. Don't let the interviewer push you around."

"Ok, but how do we maintain control during an interview? We simply answer the questions?"

"Ok, look, listen to my introduction again." I repeated what I'd written. "Now tell me what you think his next question will be?"

Kumar was expecting a question he'd already anticipated; sure enough, Gargi, said exactly that.

Gargi said "Obviously about the Gita and all-"

Now excitement in his voice, Kumar cut in. "Exactly! This way, we'll make him ask the questions we want. All the questions will be in the areas of my strength"

Gargi simply nodded. With a little more clarity on his idea, she decided to try this method. She started writing something and was completed it in a few minutes.

The interviews started after the group discussion with a panel of three people.

Kumar entered the interview cabin and found a panel of three interviewers. The two men – one just old enough to have achieved the position – and a woman inside were obviously his interviewers. The older man looked very strict.

He was tense, vigilant, and somewhat nervous when he was signalled to sit on a chair. As he sat down, he struggled to give a confident smile despite practice.

He was asked to sit and wait a minute. It was when he observed the room. This interview room was not at all dreadful as he expected. It was rather a beautiful one. The greenery was quite visible from the window on his left. Some beautiful pictures on the walls around him made the room a pleasant place. The only incongruous thing, was a pair of antlers fixed vertically crossing each other on the front wall right above the wall clock.

"Please introduce yourself Mr. Kumar" The interviewer on the right asked.

"Sir, my name is Kumar. I'm from a small town in Haryana. I'm a great believer of ancient Indian scriptures and my favourite is the Bhagwat Gita." Kumar responded with smile, despite the risk of an unconventional introducing.

The interviewer smiled to Kumar's surprise as he was the one who looked most serious among them and spontaneously asked the question he had expected: "What makes Bhagwat Gita your favourite?"

"Sir, its teachings have transformed me. I've changed from a mediocre person into someone with undaunted courage and a compassionate heart. I believe reading it turns you into a man who can maintain his composure in any turmoil. Books like Bhagwat Gita and Upanishads are truly enlightening."

"Impressive. Can you share any specific part from the Gita that you're especially fond of?" the interviewer on the left curiously asked.

"Sir, there are many, but there's one particular Shloka in the first chapter which is my favourite." He goes on to recite and elaborate its meaning.

"In this, Lord Krishna says to Arjuna: O Valorous Kshatriya, drop all your weaknesses of heart and surrender your unnecessary worries unto me instantaneously, and stand up to fight a righteous war. Only this path is auspicious for you.

"Sir, whenever I'm upset or consider giving up, this shloka inspires me to drop all negative thoughts and continue fighting my own righteous war." This time, Kumar looked straight into the eyes of all the interviewers and left a trail for them for the next obvious question.

"What do you mean by a righteous war? Being a believer in non-violence, I personally believe no war can be righteous." interviewer chuckled while trying to trip him.

"Sir, neither a war nor a peace is absolutely righteous in itself. Your purpose, your intention and the state of mind make it righteous. When Bhagat Singh sacrifices or Subhash Chandra Bose fights, it's righteous because their purpose was attaining freedom for the country. So, with a right purpose even a war becomes righteous. And those who kept silence against the torture and discrimination, were wrong. So, their peace and non-violence were inauspicious." Kumar answered elaborately and confidently.

Over the next 15 minutes, most of the questions asked were from the Gita, and other ancient scriptures. The interviewer tried many times to outsmart him by asking questions which were not knowledge based but application based, like how they helped him grow but these he was easily able to answer with real life examples. Towards the end, came the questions that briefly touched on his aim in life, future, MBA etc.

When he came out of the interview, he sent a winning smile towards Gargi, wished her luck and motivated her with: "Trust yourself. Our plan is going to work. All the best." Gargi smiled back in thanks.

Gargi too belonged to a small town in Himachal. She had gone through the same ordeals as Kumar as far as language barrier and confident speaking were concerned. She started learning English only after reaching Chandigarh. Spoken English had become a monumental undertaking. She would often cry when it would get tough.

But one moment changed it all; she was scolded by her CAT teacher for not working enough on English. The reprimand quashed her already hurt pride and pushed her to push back. She made a commitment to work with utmost sincerity from then on. She never looked back after that and worked on her written English so much so that she scored impressively. However, she was still struggling with spoken English because her major focus during the 6 months of preparation was written English alone.

Gargi's Interview:

Now the fear of poor spoken English was crippling her possibility of succeeding. She tried Kumar's idea out though, unsure about change at last moment. She still thought that you couldn't get away with hiding something from an experienced person like an interviewer. However, she'd always trusted Kumar so she made up her mind to go ahead with his idea, looked the new introduction over, practiced a little and entered the interview room.

"Would you mind introducing yourself?" Asked the interviewer.

"Sir, I'm Gargi from Himachal. I'm true to my name which means a wise and thoughtful person who inspires to think. I've seen a lot of struggles but those struggles have made me more balanced, organized, and perspicacious. I may be of average intelligence, but I've got extraordinary commitment, composure and an innovative mind, quintessential requirements to lead an organization." Gargi stated all with her Himachali accented English. She had intentionally used some high-sounding words in her sentences, having grown confident from using them through months of practice.

"How can you say that you have extraordinary commitment?" The interviewer's next question showed Gargi that Kumar was right and she relaxed.

"The most recent example is language sir. A girl from a small town in Himachal, who couldn't speak even a sentence in English just 8 months ago, is now speaking English with excellent vocabulary in her life's first interview. It started with a commitment made to my teacher at the beginning of my CAT preparation. English used to be a formidable hurdle and even now it's a weakness as you can see from my accent and pronunciation. But after my commitment I worked hard and improved my written English and you can see my score on the card for this year. Here's my last year's score too, in which I've scored so poor. You can easily compare the two." She confidently handed her two years' score cards over to the interviewer who asked the question.

"There are many other instances when I had proved myself. I would like to repeat that I may be of average intelligence and smartness, but my commitment and persistence is truly remarkable. My father always says that people achieve remarkable goals not through intelligence, but through commitment and persistence. That's why I'm quite confident of my future goals." Gargi's eyes glinted at the end of her answer, something noticed by the three across the table.

"What are you going to achieve in your life? Have you thought of something?"

Gargi relaxed the longer she stayed; one after the other, she was asked questions she'd anticipated.

"Sir, I've clearly defined my goals for next 10 years. First is an MBA from a reputed college followed by a few years' experience and then my dream in life; opening a chain of school of excellence wherein the focus will be on Math, English, Health, and fun. To achieve this, I need a team of like-minded visionaries. I'm sure that I'll find such people. In fact, I've already found one." Gargi's lucid answers left an impression on them.

"Who's that?" One interviewer asked.

"Someone who was interviewed earlier today, Kumar. He's someone with the same spark and sincerity as I. Though his goal isn't fixed yet, I've seen his inclination towards something like my dream. I believe we could be a great team." Her truthful answers displayed her conviction.

The interview lasted for a long time and its focus was on her vision. Her fear that had shrouded her confidence was easily dispelled as the interview proceeded. She realized that the interviewer was focused on her goals, vision, and life, not the language she spoke.

Post the interview, both ate the most satisfactory meal they had ever had. They discussed the same what happened inside the interview room. Gargi shared the interviewer's good wishes with Kumar, which surprised him a lot and they both laughed heartily at this.

Chapter 7

Level 2 of Successful Interviews

❖ The Treasure Chest in Daily Interactions

Nitin had asked the entire group to meet up to discuss about his interview. Sonam was also interested as her interview was also a few days away. They all decided to meet at the lake at lunch time.

"I've an interview today." revealed Nitin sadly while flipping some pages in hand.

"It's apparent from your face." Harman elbowed Kumar and everyone laughed.

"No, kidding please. Any hint about the possible questions?" Nitin was very serious.

"The previous day, Kumar learnt one important lesson about interviews which he would like to share with everyone." Gargi spoke up excitedly.

"What's that?"

"See, after yesterday's interview I'm almost hundred percent sure that Interview is an interaction, nothing more. Don't take them seriously, take them sincerely." Kumar said while taking the first sip of the cold coffee.

"Why do you think so?" Sonam promptly questioned.

"I don' think so, I know so."

"How?"

"Let's take the example of a person who can't clearly express his feelings in a general conversation. Naturally, he wouldn't be able to express himself in an interview. The same is true for a person who can't speak about his goals confidently. Now compare to someone, who generally expresses himself clearly and confidently. He'll do the same convincingly in interviews too, correct?" Kumar wondered aloud.

"So, you mean, that the one who speaks effectively in everyday life will clear the interviews. Don't you think you're over simplifying?" Harman remarked.

"Obviously! It can't be so simple. If it was, wouldn't most people clear interviews?" Nitin added his disapproval.

"Oh, come on! Those who play well in everyday games, will naturally have an edge over others and are more likely to win." Gargi defended.

"It's not just about playing well, it's also about practicing sincerely every day. If someone is careful during practice, they'll naturally be careful in an important match. It's a matter of habit, not a momentary bit of luck." Kumar added on.

"Alright, that makes sense. Chances certainly increase if one practices sincerely. It's natural." Nitin said.

"So, to simplify, interviews should be prepared for in a way that we focus on every day conversations." Parmjeet concluded.

"If we practice speaking clearly and precisely in our daily conversations, we make this a habit, which pays off for interviews." Gargi added.

"Alright. I'll share what I've learnt about interviews. Earlier I had never gone for interviews this way, I'd cower at the mention of them. As I gained experience, I improved a lot. I can tell you the following points:

1. Long before preparing for an interview, it's important that you are careful about every conversation you have in life.

2. Be observant during these conversations. Everything that an interviewer checks can be checked during these conversations if you observe yourself. Like body language, tone, eye contact, word choice, effective explanation of ideas, listening to others etc. If one develops the habit of working on these during every day conversations, they will naturally have a greater edge. The habit corrects everything and makes you confident in all conversations.

3. Approach interviews playfully and sincerely, not seriously. Most people, like I used to, get too nervous usually for no reason. A scared mind creates a delusion usually for one of two reasons:

a) You have not prepared before the interview

b) You've not done justice to your past responsibilities.

If these are corrected, the fear of interview disappears.

4. Interviewer sits there to select not reject you. Just stay calm.

5. If you're not selected, don't take it as a rejection. It's just the interviewer whose hands are tied with only a few availabilities. Many times, the interviewer can't select all those who deserve it because of the limited number of available positions. The limitation is the interviewer's not yours."

Everyone showed their appreciation by clapping. These claps held a special meaning for him since it happened in front of his beloved Gargi. He was on cloud nine.

"I totally agree with you. So, what do you suggest? Shall I improve my general conversation now. My interview is today only?" Nitin was still nervous about his own interview.

"Obviously you can't. But you can do one thing which should help you. Write down-

- Your strengths and weaknesses

- Achievements in life

- Important learnings from your big mistakes

- Why do you want to do MBA?

- Your plans for the future

Write them down in clear words and in detail. Then practice speaking them in a good flow." Gargi was confident in her advice.

"Correct. This won't take much time as some of these points would already have written in your notes. Spend more time practicing how to speak these in your answers." Kumar added while picking up the notes from the table.

"What do you guys suggest for my interview next week?" said Sonam.

"You should do both as you're too poor." Harman laughed for a moment, then stopped after Sonam's stare indicated her seriousness.

"No, she's right Sonam. You have one week to experiment with your conversational skills. We'll all help you. Simultaneously, write down all these important points along with more." Yogesh added.

"Alright. Thanks"

Sonam was so relieved after this discussion.

"Kumar and Gargi should throw a party as their interviews went well." Harman chuckled.

"Don't jinx them by saying that. Let's first wait for the result." Gargi quickly hushed Harman.

"No problem. But at least your interviews went well and you are relieved of the stress. So, we deserve a small party, something more than this cold coffee." Parmjeet spoke.

"Ok fine. Let's order cheese sandwiches and burgers."

All of them had their snack. Nitin left for his interview after that. The rest were in high spirits and wanted to celebrate more. In no time, their favourite game of songs started and everybody got into it. Their clamour and singing could be heard at a distance too. But in this celebratory mood, everyone was unaware of the surprise that awaited them.

The Twist of the Destiny

Gargi and Kumar had met each other during their CAT preparation. They were in different batches, but would meet when some combined group discussions take place. It was during one such group discussion that Kumar first noticed her, when Gargi impressed everyone with her powerful views on the topic despite using broken English.

After some days, she was again introduced by Parmjeet. It was when he personally met her for the first time. Her elegant personality, added with melodious voice, left an indelible impression on his mind. This was the first time he fell head over heels in love with someone. After a long struggle his proposal was later accepted by her.

But like in every love story, their love also had a story. A story replete with diverse experiences of disapproval, jealousy, romance, and sacrifice. Kumar would call them adventures, Gargi would calling them hindrances.

After months of being together, they knew each other inside out. Their affair was not of an ordinary girlfriend and boyfriend. It had grown into a 24-caret gold perfection, polished by frictions of adversities like non-acceptance by Gargi's family and difficulties faced during their practice for CAT and GD/PI.

So far, they had managed to go ahead with each other while keeping focus on their preparation. The success in CAT and then satisfactory performance in GD/PI, further deepened their belief that they were the right choice for each other. It strengthened their conviction towards each other.

Their friends would call them the perfect couple.

But they had no idea that perfect combinations seldom

occur. They were unaware of the imminent upheaval; Gargi's family had made up its mind.

The celebration was short-lived as for some of them their lives were going to take a sharp turn. Kumar had hardly started doing well, when fate took a perilous turn.

Gargi's phone rang just after they finished lunch. Unaware of its gravity, Gargi answered. After two minutes, she returned silently trying to hide the truth but her expressions gave her away. Noticing this, Kumar took her aside. After a while, they left without telling anyone anything. Mystery cloaked the situation leaving everyone in consternation. Parmjeet was about to stop them, but decided not to.

The next day was the official GD/PI result. Both weren't worried about it; not because of the overconfidence, neither because of the lack of seriousness. But reason was something else. There was a storm brewing, about to hit them hard.

The next day, the news of their pending separation came to everyone. It's because- Gargi's mother had fixed her marriage with someone else. This news drained all the joy of clearing the interview for both and being selected for their dream college.

They were totally shattered after this decision. Kumar didn't tell anyone about his success at the interview as he was facing a defeat at life.

Now as if this wasn't enough, Gargi decided to drop her admission. It became impossible for her to study in the same college as Kumar after the separation. When he came to know of Gargi's decision, he was shaken. He knew it very well how hard Gargi had tried for this. So, he tried convincing her to not let go of such a huge opportunity. But she was adamant, heart-broken.

He somehow withstood their break up. They had originally considered rebelling but her mother's health stopped them. Her mother was a heart patient. She had already suffered two heart-attacks; a third could prove fatal. They were both hopeful that they would peacefully convince her father first, who in turn would easily convince her mother. But both her parents didn't relent. Finally, Kumar and Gargi had to give in and promised that they won't go against their parents' wishes.

However, dropping admission was beyond what he'd anticipated. Ending their relationship was unbearable, her quitting only pushed it further. Kumar couldn't understand why she'd destroy her future like this. Her marriage had been fixed with the guy; Gargi's fiancée knew that she had secured admission. This decision of hers might also lead to the new relation breaking too. Kumar was horrified thinking of the possibilities cascading into the future.

Now after ending the relationship over her parents' wish, he decided to make an equally tough decision. He thought that instead of Gargi, he would quit. This would save her marriage, her degree, and her parents' wishes. Her reasoning to quit was that they both couldn't study together. Keeping this in mind, he decided the safest thing was to quit himself and let Gargi complete the degree. He took the necessary steps and explained everything to Gargi who was shocked to hear all this. She didn't want Kumar to sacrifice for her sake, but it was too late as he had already quit.

Within a fortnight, he'd lost his life-partner, his bright career, his MBA dream, and all hope. All his planning had fallen apart. He was down in the dumps to such an extent that he left Chandigarh and went off the grid for the next many months.

Chapter 8

Writing A Brand-New Destiny

❖   A New Future Lies In Realization

Kumar's life had completely changed after all that happened. He had quit his MBA dream and found refuge at his old friends' place, Pradeep and Silky, in Mumbai. After spending a few months in purely a distressed state, he somehow started becoming normal. He came to Gurugram and was staying with his childhood friends, who had rented a room. After a year or so, he realized that he needed to get back into his professional life to make ends meet.

The regret and frustration of not doing anything significant for the whole year, started piling up but he felt no desire to do anything. He was plagued by an inertia making it hard to move on.

Though, he was extremely thankful to all his friends who supported him during such a tough time without expecting anything in return, such a support shouldn't last long, otherwise it would ruin whatever was left of his self-respect.

"I will have to stand on my feet again." He thought.

His ambition had evaporated, no thought of achieving anything, anymore. As the time passed, old dreams would often pop up in mind, but he'd ignore them as the accompanying pain was too much. Finally, after discussing it with his friends, he started giving home tuitions and teaching at a tuition centre.

He kept going like this for a year. His old passions and dreams were long forgotten, perhaps on purpose. Now he no longer had a wish to reach any height, or earn money or fame. He only wanted a humble existence. He had become complacent in life. Nothing felt worth the effort of chasing.

Reading spiritual books became his favourite pastime. Spiritual attainments attracted him more than any other ambition. He started spending most of his time in certain spiritual practices which further pushed him away from any materialistic achievements.

At the back of the mind, he knew that something was wrong with his approach. He perhaps concealed his indolence, fears, and procrastination with the pretext of spiritual knowledge and practice. But every time such a thought popped up, he would ignore it.

He was quite happy working as a tuition teacher, this gave him enough money to sustain himself and enough satisfaction by contributing towards someone's progress. Over time, he realized that the success of his students gave him vicarious achievement, this would motivate him. But overall, he was living only a mediocre and uneventful life.

If you had a dream, and you'd chased it with commitment, you can't limit yourself to mere survival. Kumar's was the same. He was lost in his own world, not doing anything to improve his life, burying himself in living an unproductive life.

His burdened heart was a sign he was frustrated, a clear sign of the futility of trying to live peacefully. Reading the spiritual books of ancient wisdom would often make him think **"The untapped potential always leads to pain and regret."**

At times, the realization came with a deep pain, but he would never give it a second thought. Thus, it would fail to yield any result of change.

One evening, on the way back to his hometown, the panoramic view of the sky made him pull over, get out and observe divine beauty of nature. He simply absorbed the breath-taking view; the green fields surrounded by trees, the colourful evening sky, everything. The landscape grew more wooded as he approached a nearby canal lined with eucalyptus just across a sunken meadow.

He sat on a concrete perch near the canal to spend some time in the lap of nature. He noticed pearl millet seeds were scattered on the ground near him for birds. He picked up a few seeds and looked closely at them. A sudden thought crossed his mind.

"If a seed remains a seed and doesn't grow, what difference would it make to the world?" This thought reminded him of something he had read long ago in the Upanishads.

"The purpose of a seed is to bloom. If it doesn't, there's no difference between a seed and a stone. The glory of a seed is in growing into a plant and flowering, not in living like a dead stone. So, a seed is unfortunate when it doesn't grow. Similarly, the life of a human being is justified only when it grows in all possible ways."

"The purpose in life for us is to realize our full potential. If we stay constrained in our mediocre existence, we waste our life. This law of existence is one every human being must follow; we are born with immense, innate potential and a natural inclination to live an enriched, joyful life."

This thought shook him badly.

He realized, **"The way in which I am currently living-unhealthy, joyless and stagnant- is a clear reflection of the wrong way I've adopted. Am I going the unfortunate seed's way?"** The realization filled him with unease and regret.

He started to think of what the important things in his life were; his priorities, responsibilities, his way of living everything. After many years, he felt the zest of life erupt inside him again. It pushed him to find his aim. It was the first time in years he felt something so strongly.

He wanted to relieve himself of emotional storm brewing inside. It was so strong that he wanted to be alone now, not to go home. He changed the plan, informed his family of going back to Gurgaon for something urgent and turned around.

The next couple of days were filled with regret and crying. Every time a different thought would start the crying. Sometimes thinking of what all happened in Chandigarh where all his dreams dashed to the ground, other times he would find himself guilty of knowingly wasting years of his life post Chandigarh, living insignificantly since then. But these tears were perhaps melting the solid waste rocks of wrong beliefs, excuses, and perceptions about life built up inside him.

The palpable tension in the room along with the dampness due to his flooding tears was even felt by the room service. They were puzzled as to why this man had booked the room. Even the hotel manager would often find remains of tears on his face whenever he went out aimlessly and was quite sympathetic to him.

Intermittently, thoughts of what to do next would also pop up. Sometimes he would think of pursuing a dream, which would excite and puzzle him at the same time.

A few sleepless nights later he remembered a childhood dream and decided to give it a thought. The question he asked himself then started the falling dominos for the rest of his life.

"What fascinates me the most?"

A few probable answers came to mind;

- The dream of doing MBA from a premier college had died with separation with Gargi. It's too late to start it again because of financial problems, age, etc.

- Joining another Sales and Marketing job wasn't something that fascinated him.

- Since childhood he'd had a dream of speaking onstage and addressing an audience. While interesting it wasn't an actual profession.

After a while though, the same thing came back to him again and along with it a memory from his college days: Whenever he saw someone speaking on stage, something pushed him to emulate. He'd failed to recognize this dream earlier, even though it was always there. He thought how one of his seniors, Mr. Aman Thukral, was always his favourite because he was a confident speaker.

Kumar thought back to all the times he'd look for opportunities to give seminars, especially during college days.

Once he thought to give a seminar on a topic during the third year of graduation. He was excited but unfortunately, the teacher had to leave for a few days. Excitement, made it too difficult to wait until next week. So, he decided to go about it without permission from the subject teacher.

The teacher was absent and the topic had been rescheduled for the next week. But he took the class representative in confidence and delivered the seminar. It took him two days to cover the topic in detail. He also invited one of the other teachers as a guest. He was satisfied with his delivery. He got impressive feedback from the guest teacher as well as by his classmates. He was sure to receive praise from the subject teacher too next week.

He remembered how surprised he was when reprimanded by the teacher for having covered the topic in his absence.

The memory brought a smile to his face.

But all these things have no bearing on whether he should pursue this as a goal.

Will this help me achieve a bigger goal in life?

He wasn't sure but the idea enticed him.

His teacher, also an inspirational speaker, Mr. Akash Gautam, whose magical teaching, and communication skills had had a deep impact on him. He remembered that he'd always found his sessions mesmerizing.

He also thought of all his classes, some seminars, and special sessions, he attended along with his friends. Everyone would be left inspired. Even after so many years now, he could still see how that unfading impression of his teacher was still imprinted on his heart.

"So, how is it going to help me sort my quandary about what dream shall I pursue? Is it just a random thought or a relevant one?" This thought questioned the relevance of his previous thought.

"How would I get the answer to my question?" He asked himself to reach the answer.

The memory of a discourse of Sri Sri Ravi Shankar came to his mind, "Knowing yourself is the key to all wisdom. The answers to all the questions are inside you."

This prompted another question, "Have I always failed to listen to this call from within? Will I get the answer to what fascinates me the most and what is the purpose of my life from within?"

Contemplation revealed how he'd been wrong about his own life earlier. There were instances when he was extremely fascinated with speaking on stage, impacting other's lives, being an inspiration to others. He remembered every time he would attend Akash sir's sessions, he only had one thing in mind-to be like him and make an impact on hundreds of people. He remembered that since he had started teaching, the passion of addressing an audience kept poking him.

"Is it time to take this as my dream and start working on it?" Kumar asked himself sincerely.

If becoming a speaker had to be my dream, can it answer the next important question?"

"Will it lead to achieving a bigger goal, which is to leave a positive impact on people and help them achieve higher goals?"

As an answer to this clear and easy question, he realized he could lift people up psychologically, inspire them to do great things in life. He could do a great service to the nation and humanity.

The simple and clear answer sent a surge of excitement within him. Perhaps this is what he had been looking for, for years. This answer had come out as if a hidden treasure had unveiled itself.

The long pending answer to his questions and the way out of this slump left him feeling energized.

He knew that he'd found what he was seeking. He knew it's a path, not a destination. He had sought a path, more precisely a right path, which he got. His experience could tell him that it was no ordinary thing, perhaps the most important thing, which he had discovered.

All this started with a right question, "What fascinates me the most?"

Chapter 9

Asking the *Right* Questions

❖ An Art That Certainly Shows The Right Path

One right question changed his whole life. It gave him much needed 'direction' to his thoughts. This is the first time he realized the power of asking right questions.

He sat with his diary and started writing, **"You get the right answer only when you ask the right question."**

If I was asking myself incorrect questions, I was dissatisfied by the answers and kept going around in circles. The dissatisfaction from the answers created more incorrect questions and the cycle kept repeating over and over.

"This trick of asking a right question can be a game-changer." He noted.

This led to a long chain of thoughts, which he kept observing uninterrupted and noting when needed.

For example, if you want to buy a red Ferrari, you don't start with a red Ferrari. You start with wanting to buy a red, luxurious sports car. Now in this case, you might not get a red Ferrari, as there are many other luxurious sports car models. You end up spending precious time and money on something you did not exactly want, a realization that comes later.

The same applies when it comes to intangible things like a goal. Our mind is cluttered with things. There are people who are unclear about their purpose and never lead an fulfilling life. They never live a life which is fulfilling, satisfactory and joyful. Only a clear goal with a clear path will help lead such a life. This clarity comes when we ask a right question to ourselves.

Asking a right question starts you on the path of what to do.

Kumar could discover his dream when he asked a right question to himself- what fascinates me the most? After getting to know his dream, naturally the next thing he asked was- how to go about doing this? As a result, he got a clear idea about what steps he should take to reach his dream.

So, he decided to:

- polish his own language skills, especially Spoken English

- meet people and understand their career issues

- help others overcome their weaknesses and polish their strengths

He wasted no time to start working on first steps simultaneously, which were language skills and interacting with new people.

There were numerous of coaching centres for Spoken English and Personality Development courses he visited and finally picked one of the most famous in Delhi. He started classes and worked passionately on his language skills. Even after completing the course he continued practicing untiringly.

His short-term goal was to attain expertise on the language. Though he was extremely shy initially, but under the guidance of his teacher, he worked tirelessly to remove his hesitation. He also invented some novel ways of practicing English.

He would record his voice on mobile and would send to his friends, who would then either reply or give feedback. In the same way, he would listen to their voice messages too.

Slowly he improved on his language skills, but he could still clearly see that hesitation was killing his overall effectiveness. Then he decided to work on this more extensively.

He adopted a new way. He knew that it would go only when he would talk to strangers. Then he decided to visit restaurants and hotels. He promised himself to visit 100 restaurants and hotels in next 30 days and talk to them in English. He utterly failed to speak with the receptionist in his first 3 visits and came out embarrassed.

Then after his teacher's suggestion, he improvised his way by going with a scripted and practiced conversation, so that he would speak loudly and struggle less to find appropriate words.

The trick worked well. He became more confident after the 10 visits and soon he did away with the script and comfortably completed the target of 100.

At times, he would also accompany his friends and give himself a challenge of speaking loud at a public place. He would throw a party if he failed to do so.

Soon his tenacity paid off.

After a year he was confident in his language skills. Though he still felt a need to work on certain areas, at a friend's behest he started training people in spoken English at his coaching centre. Slowly he improved further and kept practicing on his own.

It took him another year to gain confidence in English. He started his own coaching centre in Delhi during his third year of training and after a few months, he opened another in Gurgaon. That's when he got around to working on the next part of his goal- 'interacting with people and understand their career issues.' As a trainer, he'd already been doing it, but now he had to do it in a more organized and dedicated way.

After meeting hundreds of students and professionals from various places he noted there was something weird happening:

- Almost everyone obsesses over wanting to speak fluent English.

- Many professionals feel crippled without spoken English despite knowledge of their subject

- School teachers and lecturers who speak English earn higher salary and are employed and retained by organizations

- No company would offer a good salary if you can't speak English

- This pressure makes countless intelligent students feel insecure

- Kids are raised with the perception that their education would be wasted without decent English

- Many students have this notion that it's English that you need primarily to succeed professionally, not skills

- Some children perceive their parents as less educated due to poor English

This information wasn't completely new to him. Hailing from a small educationally backward town in Haryana, he was familiar with the pain and ordeal of an average student. But now, on a mission to understand this to help people, he could see clearer.

He wondered about the disastrous psychological effect on him and now on the students! He realized that growing up with an inability to speak English well makes the chances of your success scanty. This impression is engrained in your mind and you are conditioned to believe that this is the only reality which leads you to closing the doors to big possibilities yourself.

However, the reality is different since your performance in an interview depends on multiple factors, but you can't see them as you have long been conditioned that way. You only see your weakness and poor English.

The worst impact of this perception is:

- You assume English something without which one's self-confidence evaporates, making people stammer, limbs shake and eventually he learns to accept defeat.

- You think English is the cause of confidence. You believe that you'll never improve unless you learn good English.

So as a result, you have two things mixed up in your mind. First, that you must learn English and second that you must gain confidence. The cluttering starts here.

To learn English, you visit a coaching centre. But you enter with the intention to learn English, not gaining confidence. So, you tend to ask wrong questions. Wrong questions like:

- How long would I take to learn English?

- Will I ever be able to speak English?

- Will I be able to groom my personality with this course?

- What will you teach me in this course (syllabus etc.)?

He smiled thinking that confidence can't be gained by simply learning English or any other language. If you speak Hindi with low confidence, you would naturally speak English with same type of confidence. Language has nothing to do with your self-confidence.

He realized that instead of English, people want to-

- Gain great confidence in speaking (Not a specific language).

- Have confidence to clear interviews

- Express themselves fearlessly during a group discussion

- Speak on stage without a stammering

- Talk convincingly during conversations

He realized that people need to have a clear picture in their mind that they need to gain confidence. This leads to the right questions that people should ask:

-Will I be able to become a confident speaker?

-Will I be an effective communicator after this course?

-What should I do to be able to speak fearlessly?

He thought about his training to help his trainees find answers to these questions and help them work it out.

One day a trainee asked him "How to gain confidence during a presentation?"

Kumar responded with another question:

- How do you gain confidence to face a fast bowler in a cricket match?

  Or

- How do you gain confidence to drive a car?

By facing the fast bowler or driving a car in real life. The more you face a bowler or drive a car the more comfortable and confident you become. The process is gradual and takes time." He answered emphatically. The same is true for gaining confidence in speaking. Put yourself in situations which challenge you."

"Could you please share how you resolved your issues in spoken English? You'd said earlier your English was also very poor and you were extremely shy." Asked another trainee.

"I used to be shy since childhood. Forget speaking on stage, I couldn't even talk to a stranger. This fear hampered all my progress. I grew into a person who didn't like taking risks. Even to approach a person, I would think many times. Another tendency of being bothered too much about others' opinions developed. I never realized the kind of damage I did to myself. But, **Awareness is the first step in transformation."** Kumar Paused for a second and continued with a smile.

"When realization struck, I decided to change. At first, I didn't know how to go about it. Like many people, I chose a coaching centre and started learning Spoken English. My fluency and my confidence also improved yet it didn't give me what I actually wanted."

"Then what did you want?"

"I wanted to be a confident speaker who could speak on stage, addressing a large gathering fearlessly. Learning English helped me speak another language but the fear of public speaking still followed me. English only helped a little with confidence. Gaining confidence for public speaking is an entirely different exercise from learning Spoken English.

"I realized that by working on Spoken English, one can improve only spoken English. But if I want confidence, I need to do things which would build confidence by practice in situations that make me nervous. This simplification transformed me from a timid speaker to a confident speaker."

Kumar smiled, "So, remember- If you want to gain confidence, do something that makes you confident. Start with a small challenge and build up to tougher ones."

Chapter 10

Speaking- The Preeminent Skills

❖ **A journey to mastering the master of all skills**

After interacting with hundreds of people Kumar realized- **Speaking is a common art, yet rarely mastered.** Everybody does it, but not everybody is confident about it. Kumar realized this was a common weakness with a widest number of professionals. His own experience told him the same thing.

He penned down this conclusion based on his recent observations:

- Speaking is the common-most thing among human beings

- Effective communication is ironically uncommon

- Most people recognize its great power, yet don't work on it

- Those who do, transform themselves from ordinary to extraordinary

One question intrigued him a lot, "If speech is such a common skill, why is it that some people leave an unforgettable impression on your mind when they speak, while many others fail to do so?

He shut his eyes and slouched on a chair thinking about the right answer. A memory flashed in his mind.

Kumar and his friends gathered to attend a seminar in Chandigarh. They sat in the last row of the hall as they were late. The speaker, Mr. Akash Gautam, a renowned motivational speaker, and their teacher, had organized this seminar. The seminar finished in a scintillating fashion and the hall echoed with thundering applause and a standing ovation. After exiting the hall, Kumar spoke to his friends, "How can someone speak so well! I am mesmerized!"

Parmjeet's response stayed in his mind ever since- **"It's not what you say, but how you say it that matters."**

"What shortcoming do you guys see in my way of speaking? I'm eager to improve on this skill."

"As such there isn't any. But I would love to suggest you something that will help you for sure." replied Harman with seriousness.

"What's that?"

"You should always keep quiet."

Kumar elbowed her playfully while both Parmjeet and Harman burst into laughter.

This memory brought a smile on his face as he sat up holding his pen back in hand. The idea was indelibly ingrained in his mind.

This led to the search for the answer of-**What's the difference between an ordinary and extraordinary speaker**?

He thought that the answer lay with people with huge fan followings or those who impacted others with their words.

He chose speakers in different fields and decided to observe them carefully:

- Spiritual leaders

- Trainers and Motivators

- Teachers

- News anchors

- Experts speaking on TV

- Politicians

After a lot of observation, he found similarities amongst them despite their differences. It showed him that effective speech lay in basic things. If these basics are practiced, one can transform the way they speak.

Almost all powerful speakers were:

- **GENUINE**:

  They were genuinely concerned about their listeners' progress, when they talked to you, they manifested that concern and won your heart.

- **INSPIRING:**

The most effective were those who practiced what they spoke. Their very presence becomes inspirational and their talks help your spirit rise through the ceiling and you feel inspired.

- **AMIABLE:**

  They're available without being too available to the public. Simply, they don't keep giving 'gyan' all the time, rather they push you to action. After an interaction, you decide what change to make.

- **JUST:**

  Indiscriminate contact from both their side and yours. They never impose their views or advice on you, you connect without pressure from their side

- **TIME MACHINE:**

  In a 2-step process they act as a time machine to take you to future. First, they show you a better and promising future. Next, they make you believe that you can easily reach it. In their presence, you can break the shackles that hold you back and help you rise above.

He decided to inculcate these qualities in his speeches to become a powerful speaker. He attended another seminar of another renowned speaker, Mr. Arfeen Khan and understood one crucial point. He said, **"You don't need to be a 'showman' to be a great speaker.** No boasting, no shouting, no high-sounding words are necessary. You can be purely genuine and simple in speaking."

This made it easier to show and be a powerful speaker.

One day after a training session, he had a one-on-one with a student who'd approached him for a discussion over some issues related with personality. The student was a post-graduate with a bright academic record, but he'd failed the campus recruitment and as a result he'd lost confidence and was dispirited. Kumar completed the session early, with the start of a plan to help the student which started with the question; **"What about the many who don't have a high level of confidence and belief? Is there any way to help them cultivate it?"**

He wanted to help others. He felt that the kind of ordeal he'd faced in his life was easily evitable, provided someone knew how.

So, he wondered, about the factors affecting the minds of people, especially students and new professionals.

"Could traits like confidence and belief be adapted in someone in order to change the course of their life?"

He kept these thoughts in mind while interacting with people of different ages, backgrounds, and aspirations, specially the college students and people in the initial years of their professional life.

He related these questions with the way he had improved in his own life. He remembered how shy he was during his college years, which negatively impacted his campus recruitment and many other interviews post college.

Then he also remembered how he made progress and what factors, including friends, his commitment, and timely decisions, determined his progress when he got job after preparing for interviews, performed well in job, cleared CAT, and finally got admission in a premier B-school.

He put together some key factors to excel in life and noted them down:

- right routine

- right environment

- right choice

"Some people are able to control these factors, but the majority is too distracted." He thought.

Though some people thought luck was an important factor in success, he decided it wasn't since it's not tangible or certain. Interestingly, most people knew these key points, but rarely did they use it to make their dream come true.

This led him to working on how these factors that commonly affected people. After analysing a little more, he found that three factors created four kinds of darkness in life-

- Dark Core

- Dark Pathway

- Dark Surrounding

- Dark (Blind) Driving.

Kumar shared all these in his next session with his trainees. He further elaborated these dark areas to his students.

- **DARK CORE**- LACK OF ENTHUSIASM:

  I met a batch of final year engineering students who were worried and unsure of their own capabilities. A horrible situation because if four years of your engineering studies made you so worried, why pursue it? The purpose of your studies wasn't to become a depressed person.

  Upon graduating a student should be ready to apply their knowledge and skills. If they sank into anxiety, uncertainty, and doubts, then this raises a serious question about the meaningfulness of that degree and that student's future-readiness. The future of such a student is bound to be wobbly.

Lack of enthusiasm is one of the worst ailments one can suffer from. This situation is common among the freshly graduates unfortunately, which is unacceptable. Unfortunately, this situation has been accepted as normal.

"Law of attraction says that a 'low energy' person attracts worries, disturbances and distractions." He spoke emphatically.

Such a person is likely to discontinue any dream project. So, the reverse must be true too-the more enthusiastic a person, the more he is likely to attract hope, support and helping hand and thus complete any dream project. **So, enthusiasm is a precursor to a focused, energetic, and result-oriented journey."**

- **DARK PATHWAY**- UNAWARE OF PRIORITY AND FOCUS:

Most college students waste their education doing useless things. They're given various projects to complete, numerous subjects to study for their syllabus. They waste significant time in stuff like gossip, internet browsing and games, social media, unnecessary arguments etc. However, students are seldom encouraged or guided to work on themselves. **The most successful people say that in life, the most important project is working on 'self.'** That's why such people spend time in becoming an awesome personality complete with confidence and essential skills.

On the other hand, students are encouraged to not shift their focus from in class subjects making transforming their personality, creativity, productivity etc. things of a child's daydream.

Kumar shared about his own life, "It took me all 4 years of my graduation in pharmacy to realize that I'm not made for the pharmaceutical field. I took another 4 years while working in this field to realize what I was made for. If someone had told me earlier that my top priority was to find my passion and strengths, it would've saved my several years and enormous amounts of energy which were spent doing aimless things."

 A trainee asked, "How do you feel when you see the same phenomenon around, like people unaware of their strengths, weaknesses and even aim in life?"

"It's not very strange. But it's painful because I don't want that to happen to others. A little awareness and guidance can change a whole life. You have to find your strength, your best qualities and purpose of life else your pathway remains dark irrespective of the direction you move.

One needs to make it a priority. If one could do that, half the battle is won and the other half will be as easy as pie, i.e. full of energy, joy, success and inner fulfilment.

- **DARK SURROUNDING**- Your comfort zone is your grave:

One of the biggest mistakes a student makes is to stay in the same environment. Others call it comfort zone, I call it a 'grave zone'. If we stay there, it cripples progress without us even realizing it. The environment has a profound and subtle effect on our mind. It's a deciding factor for success.

Your environment must be such that it pushes you towards your dream."

Here Kumar paused, recalling his father's words, "*If you spend most of your time with dancers, you can't be a good cricketer. Your surrounding matters a lot.*"

"What if you don't find anyone from your own field." One student asked cheekily.

"In that case let me share a Sufi proverb- *It's better to be alone than to be with 'whoever'.*" Kumar answered.

"Beware, however sweet and lovely your old friends seem, your top priority is your dream. This doesn't mean that you kick them out of your life. It means you embrace a disciplined life where your time, focus and energy are dedicated to achieving your dream. When you spend time with people with a similar interest, your focus and competitiveness increase manifold."

- **DARK DRIVING**- UNAWARE OF RIGHT HABIT OR ROUTINE:

I give you one magical way, "If you have a great dream, change your routine immediately. Otherwise it's impossible to achieve. Dreams are achieved by being what you dream to be."

"For example, if I decide to have six packs abs, I can't spend my days with the same routine as earlier. I must start a new routine where I would follow the recommended diet and exercise. Keeping the old routine means achieving the same old result."

Kumar, paused. "So, enough of darkness." A sudden change in the voice surprised the students, "We'll talk about removing this darkness in the next session." Giggles filled the room with positive vibes.

Chapter 11

Brightening Life by Illuminating the Dark Areas

❖ Becoming the Source of Energy

"Can someone tell the best way to remove darkness?" Kumar asked in a loud voice while entering the room.

"By switching the light on or lighting a candle" said students in chorus.

Kumar smiled before responding the obvious.

"The only way to remove darkness is to illuminate the area. So, all these four dark areas we discussed the day before have to be illuminated in order to remove darkness from our life. Let's brighten all the dark areas with the following.

- **BRIGHTEN THE CORE-**

  Be Enthusiastic:

  Feel enthusiastic about working on yourself. Exercise helps to a great extent in staying active and enthusiastic the entire day. Fill your mind with the energy and excitement to achieve your dream daily.

- **BRIGHTEN YOUR PATHWAY-**

  Discover your 'P's and Polish them:

  'P' stands for-purpose, passion, power (strength) and priority. These help you find your dream and focus more on work. This is of highest importance.

- **BRIGHTEN YOUR SURROUNDING:**

Here you have two options. Either

  - you change your environment from unsupportive to supportive

OR

  - you better leave for a better environment

If you value your dream, you need to do either of the two. You can't polish your 'P's as long as you stay among wrong people in wrong environment. That's the reason why almost all successful people in the world are those who leave their original place and go to new areas.

- **BRIGHTEN YOUR DAYS:**

You've had enough delays and procrastination and seen their poor result. Now it's time adopt a new routine to shape your tomorrow.

Keep telling yourself that "It's my dream, I will go for it."

"Value your dream...if you don't, who would?"

Many people have dreams. It's very common. You are not the only wise person. However, only one in a million is committed to their dreams.

For example, so many people with bad health know the reason behind it, poor physical exercise, and incorrect diet, yet they're reluctant to work on fitness to fix it. They wait until a major ailment strikes and the doctor advises them to add exercise to their routine and strictly avoid something they were eating.

Friends, please listen to my questions carefully and look for an honest answer to each of these:

- Have you identified those important areas in your life where you need to improve?

    - If yes, do you delay working on it?

    - If no, have you identified why you're unable to accomplish them? Targets set by you, then dropped?

"Kumar, sometimes we do, sometimes we don't. But is there a way to closely examine ourselves to get the result and how not to lose your momentum?" Asked another trainee.

"Definitely. There could be many. I'll share one. ***Be the source, not the seeker of Energy.***"

He continued only once all had absorbed the statement.

"Let me tell you something. One day while sitting with my mom in the drawing room with the TV on, a spiritual guru came on some channel. My mom is a big fan of listening to their speeches. She has five favourites though, she hears one or two of them religiously, while to others occasional.

That day one of my mom's most favourite saint was live. He said something I found extremely meaningful. He said, "The tragedy of the world is that people spend their golden years earning money and consuming things as much as they can. In the absence of spiritual knowledge, they ignore their responsibility to develop good health by developing self-restraint through right habits of eating, sleeping and working out along with their job and family. As a natural consequence of this ignorance, in their forties and fifties they develop physical and psychological ailments and they spend the same money they earned to get treatments. What can be more foolish! Spending your whole youth just to come back to square one!"

These words hit me very hard. I quickly realized what I was doing to myself. It wasn't that my dream was wrong, but it was my ignorance of physical and mental health. I had no discipline in eating, exercising or sleeping. Over time, it started taking a toll on my health. Often, I felt run down, there were days when I did nothing being completely exhausted. I realized that I'd never realize my dream due to losing health. In short, I realized that fitness is indispensable for a bright future. It's no use to have millions and a serious disease."

After class Kumar picked up where he'd left off in the notebook. "I had perhaps found the code to effective work-level of energy in your body."

Here he recalled the same in some of the famous speakers he observed earlier. He was stunned to see that they could speak for the whole day without the slightest sign of tiredness. He attended a few seminars which started at 9 am and continued till mid-night, when the organizers had to request the speaker to call it a day. Their own energy would raise the audience's energy too.

The next question naturally becomes, **"How would I attain a similar energy level? And what's the secret behind such inexhaustible flow of energy?"**

This question led him to the harder part-finding the answer.

One evening, on TV he saw an interaction between Mr. Obama and Mr. Modi. One channel said that Mr. Obama appreciated Mr. Modi's high energy, another showed data about how many rallies he had addressed in a day. Kumar was startled to find that there were days when he had addressed more than three rallies, at different locations. He watched some of the clippings of these rallies and was amazed by the high energy in all the rallies throughout the day.

He also watched the PM Modi's interview on a news channel who said that during his overseas visits he seldom slept in that country. Rather he chose to sleep while traveling to save time. Kumar was awestruck listening to this. The urge to have a similar energy level grew even stronger in him.

Another event that inspired him was when Milind Soman, a famous model and actor, successfully completed world's toughest race- Triathlon and won the title of 'Ironman' in 2015. That was the first time when he'd had heard of any such event. He came to know that it's an event of three consecutive challenges, 3.8 km of swimming, 180 km of cycling and 42 km of running in that order. Incredibly Milind completed this challenge in 15 hours and 19 min in his first attempt. What astonished him was to know that his accomplishment occurred at the age of 50.

Out of curiosity, he started reading more about him. He found that although Milind is widely regarded as an epitome of fitness in India, his journey there hadn't been as easy as he made it out to be. For a decade between the age of 28 and 38, he admits to having smoked up to 36 cigarettes a day. Though he'd gotten into the habit in his late twenties, it took him three years to kick it and finally quit smoking at 41 proving **it is never too late to do what you really want to**.

Kumar shared the same with his trainees, "The achievement of Milind Soman amazed me. I realized how important it is to work on some crucial areas in our life. I worked on my professional skills for a long time. I'd been chasing my dream for a few years, and already overcome my limitations. But it was just my professional life.

Professional life can't be the foundation of an entire life. The foundation lies in the basics like fitness, emotional wellness, and relationships among many others. Professional life is only a pillar in a building, one whose strength determines if you could erect a tall building or not. However, our health and relationships are the foundation, whose strength ensures basic safety, wellness, and happiness.

I understood some things from this:

- Fitness comes when we work on it

- How much, depends on how much work on it

- It takes regularity to improve fitness. Irregular efforts don't give results.

- An extremely fit and energetic body is a prized possession.

- Every passing year increases the importance of fitness. The sooner you realize it, the better it serves you.

- It tremendously improves the quality of your entire work and life.

And last but not the least; ***Being a poor man with a fit body is worth more than being a rich man with a sick body.***

Back at home, in his notebook he added the point for himself, "To realize my dreams, I need to work on being the source of energy in order to determine-

- how far I'd go (the quantitative progress)

- how well I'll move (the qualitative experience of his journey)

Below that in big letters headed **"Fitness is the key to get rid of my slow pace, frequent mood-swings, off and on popping up of health issues, and poor stamina."**

This clarity made him excited. The cure-all to most of his problems lay right before him. A new sense of confidence and clarity filled his thought process. He saw himself clearly living his dream life replete with enthusiasm and optimism.

Chapter 12

Engineering an Energetic Body

❖ **Simple 5 Steps to attain High Fitness**

He started putting effort into getting fit. He'd exercise daily, running, swimming, yoga etc. something every day.

He observed his progress over a few months and looked at the results to know what worked and didn't work. He exercised only 4 or 5 days a week, so he wasn't regular. While his fitness improved, he wasn't happy with the overall progress.

After introspection he remembered– **"Irregular efforts give mediocre result."** Which lead to him to conclude he needs to put regular efforts to get the result he wants.

He asked himself the following questions and wrote them down in the diary:

- Sometimes I work hard to achieve my goals and sometimes I don't. There are days when I work tirelessly for my dream, and there are also days (or longer) when I don't do anything at all along with the beautiful excuses.

- Sometimes I'm bursting in excitement about my goal. But it soon disappears and I'm left wondering where it's gone.

- Sometimes I'm clear about my target and stay focused. But within a few days of working, I find many reasons to quit, calling it either unrealistic or unimportant.

In a few days, he observed a similar pattern with others during his interactions.

"Is it a common issue?" He thought for a moment and continued writing.

- Your journey starts with a great excitement and determination. Within a few days, the bubble bursts and the energy dissipates, turning determination into speculation of whether your path is the right or not.

- The same thing happens with New Year's Resolutions. The initial excitement defuses soon.

Then he went back to the previous entries in the diary, where he had written about the state of mind of the new graduates and professionals. He wanted to relate his own state of mind with others', to see if he could figure out something important.

He found that a large chunk of people fell into any one of these three categories:

- Unhappy

- Very unhappy with their current job, studies, or life

- Depressed

Obviously, most people are dissatisfied with their life. Although extreme cases of depression, constitute some percentage of a great bulk of people who live with some level of dissatisfaction. There are fleeting moments of happiness and enthusiasm, but largely it's a dissatisfied mediocre life. And the reason lay in within.

He gave it a serious thought to what they must be doing, something which is antagonistic to happiness. Now there could be two things:

- **they're not doing something right**

- **they aren't stopping something wrong**

Habits or tendencies can siphon your time, energy, and money or fill you with them.

This made it as simple as a simple mathematics. If the right habits give a certain result in the future, it means that what I am today is a clear result my past habits.

This also meant the solution lay in daily routine. An unhappy present means wrong routine and habits in the recent past.

He thought, "Whatever I am today is a result of my routine of the past. For example, how I spent my last 30 days or a year, has shaped me how I am today. The more recent the greater influence on me."

"It's not what I did, but what I've been doing will shape what I will be." He noted.

In the next session with his trainees, he announced, "If someone wants to have an impressive result in the future, he must essentially have an impressive routine until he achieves it. This means one needs to think of how to change his or her routine."

"So, let me share with you my extremely simple and effective 5-step formula, which has immensely helped me achieve my target and become highly fit person."

5 Steps system towards Snowballing your Energy:

"Friends, let's compare life with travelling. If we take a trip by car, we need fuel for the car, a destination, prepare ourselves and then we enthusiastically start. The same applies to achieving your targets.

Reach a destination joyfully by taking following 5 steps:

- **Fuelling**

- **Destination Selection**

- **Choreographing or making up your mind**

- **Starting your journey**

- **Improvisation of plan**

"So, let's discuss this in detail.

- **Fuelling**:

Like how before a journey, a vehicle requires

fuelling and a mobile requires charging, you also require to fuel yourself up to achieve higher goals. How does one do this?

- Waking up early, daily exercise, yoga, meditation, a balanced diet, reading books, conversations with great people, helping someone etc., help you fuel yourself

- Discipline, Energy, Mental strength, Focus, Peace. These are the essential things that make you fit to achieve any target. It increases your quality of work remarkably.

In addition to this, I've experienced a palpable positivity and serenity in the early morning hours. Some of the best ideas come at this time. You may try if it works the same for you."

"If you are on the path to achieving Awesomeness, your physical, emotional and mental health must be your first priority. It will help you get a kick-start, leading to a greater momentum and lasting longer. You may regret choosing an uncooperative life-partner or a bad friend or a wrong college or job, but trust me you will never regret your decision of adopting these things into your routine."

- **Destination Selection**:

Imagine sitting in a car when you don't know where to go, and yet expecting to reach a destination! Isn't it insane? We do the same to our future.

Even the GPS in our mobile phones, asks for destination before it shows you the shortest way.

REMEMBER: **Unclear plans give you unclear result.**

Choose your target or goal (both short term and long term) with clarity so that you can easily find the shortest and the most convenient path. (Remember we discussed that if you want a red Ferrari, ask for a red Ferrari only, not a red luxurious sports car. So be specific).

- **Choreographing Your Mind**:

All achievers choreograph their mind to help them think clearly and move fearlessly. Choreographing your mind means taming and training your mind, else it will get distracted.

Ancient scriptures tell us our mind is our biggest enemy and our best friend. It depends on how we train it. If your mind is not in harmony with your plan you are bound to fail soon.

Choreograph, or train, your mind to accept that-

- Your goals are feasible. Your sustained focus and efforts will lead you it.

- Your strengths are real. Your mind must recognize undoubtedly that using them leads to your goal.

- Your plan is important to you. And you are not going to compromise it with distractions.

Train your mind daily so that they become the part of your subconscious. Once it's done, you will find your mind helping you like your best friend. Lying to your mind is pointless. If you are not persistent in focus, your mind will create distrust. That distrust will soon derail you from your path. Don't try to fool it, rather show it that your decision along with your efforts is real. It will take a few weeks for it to take it as real. Be patient.

- **Kick-starting your Journey**

    Your journey must have a kick-start. It's like a satellite launch, maximum energy is consumed at the beginning. Similarly, the initial days should be with great energy and total focus.

- **IMPROVISATION:**

Don't improvise before 50 days because, most

probably, such a desire is a ruse of your tricky mind to deviate you from the newly adopted routine. After 50 days your routine is strong and your mind knows better what amendments or improvisation are needed.

Chapter 13

The Super 50 Days

❖ **A Full-Proof Plan To Kick-Start Your Journey**

One day Kumar asked his trainees a strange question. "If you had to choose out of these, what would it be?

An Everlasting Smile or Suffering?

Fitness or Illness?

Creativity or Dumbness?

Courage or Cowardice?

Freedom or Imprisonment?

Compassion or Arrogance?

Before you answer, let me tell you that it's obvious to choose the first column. Now the next question, what would everybody on Earth choose?

"The first column." replied everyone in chorus.

Now the most important question, "Look around, your family members, neighbours, relatives, and all acquaintances in their 30s, 40s, older, anybody and everybody; what do you think they have in life majorly, the first or second column?"

"The second." another reply in chorus with intermittent laughter.

"Now what do you think your future holds, the former or the latter?"

"The second." replied everyone looking at each other in surprise and wonder.

"Do you think these are a result of our own choices and decisions or destiny?"

The answer this time was mixture of the both while some kept quiet.

Kumar explained, "Almost all events in life are the product of our choices and decisions. These are not something we get, but something we seed initially, which later fruit. The one who has the first set of qualities appears to have mastered his life. It is indeed the case, but what we forget is that these qualities evolve from effort, not due to fate or destiny or anything else."

Kumar looked around the hall. Some trainees were agreeing with the statement. Some were not and were whispering with the persons sitting next to them.

"Let's understand the key to an awesome life." Kumar spoke emphatically looking at those who seemed to be unsure.

What happens to us is mostly a result of what we have caused. It means most of what happened in our life happened not because they were pre-destined, but because we made them happen. It means we're the creators of destiny, not the receiver of predetermined.

Confused a student asked, "Kumar, what do you mean by choice and decision. Please elaborate."

"When I said- 'your choice and decision' what I mean is that it's not just decisions alone, but also your choices- choice of actions."

Some trainees were getting the whole idea, while some others stared cluelessly at him so he decided to try something else.

"Ok, let's understand this with an example:

Suppose one day I decide to eat some delicious, but unhealthy, food. I made a choice, and did it. Next day again, I eat junk food and feel happy. Then again, the next day. Slowly a habit develops and this craving starts becomes worse. The more I feed the habit, the worse it becomes over time. In no time I've got this new unhealthy habit. As time passes, I get the effects in the form of inactivity, laziness, obesity, or illnesses.

Now suppose I decide to eat a balanced diet and regularly exercise. I start following a routine. Slowly I develop this new habit (although it takes longer to form a good habit than a bad habit). Now I'm bound to get its effects over time in the form of activeness, stamina, higher energy, good health etc."

"So, the results we get in life, is the result of what we've chosen and decided in the past. I loved this idea!" Concluded a trainee excitedly.

"Is it applicable in other areas of life too?" asked another trainee.

"You to answer this question." Kumar said with a smile.

"Obviously. The same is true for all areas of our life like career, family, friends, relationships etc." Said some other students after taking some time to think.

"That means if we have to transform ourselves, we shouldn't wait for the destiny to do it, but we should just go for it after making a plan?"

"Obviously, we should just go for it. I liked what you said in the end- after making a plan. So, there could be many ways, but a correct way helps us more effectively." Kumar continued while the trainees nodded.

"There is a wonderful way, which worked for me and many others, that gave almost sure shot result. I call it- 50 Days formula or Super 50 Days for Awesomeness" Kumar slowly revealed a new key to the trainees.

"Sounds impressive" exclaimed a few trainees with joy.

"I'll unveil it in the second half after lunch. Be patient. See you." Kumar completed his session enthusiastically.

Everybody settled down when they saw Kumar coming from a distance.

"Avoid this great mistake and get a transformation in life as a reward." Kumar loudly stated as he entered the training room." Some students looked around as if someone has made a mistake. After finding nothing, they looked back at Kumar.

"While working on your dream, don't stop just to rest after a week or two. This feeling might arise after a few days of starting the work. It is nothing but our tricky mind nostalgic about our old routine. My own experience says that the second and the fourth week are the deadliest where most people stop their new routine and thus quit their dreams. Believe me you don't need any rest if you enjoy it. At least, not within 50 days of starting, unless recommended for certain specific targets, where your coach or guide wants you to.

"I share something very precious with you"- Kumar moved from the centre of the hall to the front.

"Just a few weeks ago, I thought of working on fitness and make it challenging. So, I decided to create a group 'Super 50 Days for Super Fitness'.

I invited more than 200 people to join the group with a simple task; a regular exercise of your choice for 50 days. If one misses a day, he or she could either leave the group or start again by counting the next day as the first day. Whoever completed the task would be a 'Fitness Icon' on everybody's social media account.

50 people joined the group and accepted the challenge. The result was as expected. I observed the pattern

which showed interesting results. The second week proved to be the worst, when most people missed a day or two as a result of which 16 people left the group, 12 decided to restart and the rest continued with a promise of showing better determination for rest of the days. Those who didn't miss a day in the second week, completed the third week with no problems.

The next deadliest was the 4th week, when everyone except 4 missed at least one day. As a result, 10 more people decided to quit and 20 decided to restart.

Out of 50 only 24 were left and out of these 24 only 4 were able to maintain strict discipline from the day one. Those who left the group, admitted that they were unable to exercise regularly. Out of the remaining 24, another 16 quit in the 6th week citing certain reasons. In the seventh week only 8 were left including the four who hadn't missed a day from the beginning. The other 4, missed only 2 or 3 days in those 50 days.

The result of the task was the most rewarding for those 8. We observed a huge impact in our fitness and energy level. We were filled with great boost of energy and confidence because we achieved what we'd committed. So, one doesn't need rest unless you're doing something where you are recommended to take rest after certain periods, like in some cases of body building exercises." Kumar took a pause for a moment.

This task also helped most of us to strengthen our decision making.

This led me to devise a simple 5 Step formula. Later this 5-point formula helped me achieve big goals. My decision to make my life grand did not go in vain. It helped me:

- stick to my plan

- create a routine that kept me on-track and supported my belief that I was doing something for my goal

- it ensured time-bound actions to calibrate right actions

- it gave me a chance for continuous improvement

- it sustained a sense of achievement by achieving something daily

So, this is how it benefitted me in my journey." Kumar completed with a wide smile.

"But don't you think it's an over-simplification of the whole matter. Because there are times when you get unlucky. Sometimes you genuinely can't follow your dreams because of certain compulsions or unavoidable other priority." A trainee responded politely.

"You are right dear. However, this simple 5 step formula helps you become more determined and chase your dreams more stubbornly. If you're unlucky once or twice, with greater determination you don't give up easily and start again. Don't you remember there were people in the task who restarted from day 1 after missing a day, while some others decided to quit. The former ones are those who are more determined. And such tasks make you more determined." Kumar explained the point with greater clarity.

"Correct. The purpose of the task is not to always win. It was to attain a great health with committed efforts. Whether you do it in one attempt or two, doesn't matter." said a trainee enthusiastically.

"Secondly, about luck, I also found that as you decide something with conviction, your destiny also responds to your decision. It starts taking a new shape and it beats to the rhythm of your clear mindset. This slowly makes you the creator of your destiny because you achieve what you decide. You own your life because you are the master now." Kumar continued with a greater conviction.

"This is how I became the creator of my destiny. I'm not saying this out of arrogance, but out of conviction that this system has made me confident enough to do what I decide and get the result.

We've all heard the phrase 'God helps those who help themselves.' This is one way to help ourselves.

With this a new triumphant spirit started pushing me beyond my limits. I started my new journey of life with a great enthusiasm.

One example, after interacting people, I came to know that my poor spoken English was a formidable barrier. Because this shortcoming had hurt me several occasions during interactions with high profile people and facing interviews. I went from being the victim of the common public perception to breaking it. Though it seems stupid now, but it was something which affected me deeply during my initial years.

I knew that English as a language has nothing to do with the qualities of a person. If I'm a dishonest person, I will stay dishonest even after learning English. Similarly, if I don't obey laws, I'm an irresponsible citizen, irrespective of whether I know English or not. But aside from such common-sense reasoning, the perception in people's mind is that English is indispensable to appear educated, talented and modern." Kumar completed that day's session with this discussion.

Chapter 14

Speak Out Fearlessly

❖ **Embarking On A Dream Journey**

One day after a session, he sat in the office chair recalling the day's important event, helping a bunch of university students prepare for Interviews. The students looked sincere but anxious. They reminded him of his own past when he was looking for some miracle to secure the job without the interview.

Kumar thought of the many students suffering from the same psychological ailment. He decided to help them.

It took him a few days more to figure out what to do. He wanted to speak from stage as his dream and to help people. Thus, he decided to combine his dream and passion; service and education- Seminars plus Training.

He looked excited with the sheer brilliance of this idea and the enormous possibilities, which it may lead to.

His idea about his dream and to help others prepare for Interviews and other public presentations slowly snowballed into a whole new program. He named this program with its aim in mind-*Speak Out Fearlessly.*

He was clear about the outcome he wanted for those who joined. He wanted his trainees to be powerful speakers so they could interact with everyone effectively, not just an interviewer. He included everything in the program that might help them in their life and make them independent and confident. Apart from interviews, group discussions, presentations, speaking on stage and public speaking were also to be part of training.

He first decided to start on the safe side and start with the small events. He held several smaller events at various school classes, college classes, private coaching centres etc. He kept the topics relevant to the needs of the students. He listed a few topics which students and professionals need the most. He decided to research them so that he could help greater number of students. The topics were:

- Learning effective Spoken English

- Gaining confidence in group discussions and presentations

- Finding your dream

- Chasing your dream

- Building an impressive personality

- Making your body language powerful

Within a year, he held more than 40 sessions and interacted with more than 1000 students.

Every session was unique in terms of its feedback. Each session made him more confident about the matter he delivered. He realized that this one year had given him tremendous experience and knowledge. It was more than he'd learnt in his whole life. It dawned on him how deep rooted these issues were amongst people, a painful reminder of his own journey.

Once he asked a final year engineering student to come on stage and talk about his best qualities in a loud voice. Forget speaking loudly the student started trembling. He would've fainted if Kumar hadn't asked him to go back to his seat. These instances further encouraged him to be more creative and find ways to help such students out. This would also help him grow into a more skilled trainer and speaker.

He also realized an insidious vacuum of skills in India. There's a mounting gap between what is taught at schools and colleges and what is required practically in people's professional lives. He was saddened by the fact that most people are poorly skilled and the worst part was abysmal communication skills. He was more sensitive about this area because this was an extremely crucial area where anyone can improve. Yet people hardly try to improve it. As a result, there is plethora of coaching institutes and online platforms emerging, where students learn English but fail to transform into powerful communicators.

This dismal picture would often prick him and push him to work harder to help as many people as possible improve their skills. So, he kept holding more sessions on all the important topics.

Meeting an unknown wise man:

He had made great strides towards becoming a powerful speaker. However, his initial definition of a powerful speaker suddenly changed after meeting a wise old spiritual man on a journey to Rishikesh. That person's face remained fresh in his mind forever.

Earlier, Kumar had only wanted to be a popular speaker, but after talking to him, he changed his mind. Earning and travelling the world used to fascinate him, however his understanding about life and success were changed after an interaction with this old man. After a short discussion, the old man came to know that he wanted to become a famous speaker. Then the old man said something that changed everything.

"Do you want to stay in the race for long?" He gazed straight at Kumar, adding a deeper meaning and gravity to the question. His first instinct was to ignore the question.

But the man's body-language and eye-contact were too compelling to ignore. Finally, he gave in, "Obviously. Everybody would say yes."

However, in his mind he knew that he didn't have a clear answer to the question. "Your answer doesn't seem genuine. Are you normally like that or is it a favour to me?" This man asked sarcastically. Embarrassed, Kumar knew he couldn't ignore the man.

"I'm sorry I sound rude. But I haven't thought about it yet." He replied.

"Ok, I'll tell you something about great speakers but only if you're interested." He said knowing the answer.

"It will be an honour to hear the answer" came the humbled response.

His unforgettable response stayed in his mind, "Great speakers are ordinary people infused with extraordinary genuineness, fearlessness and steadfastness. They are those who make a positive impact on the life of others. So, don't run after money or fame, to stay long, make an impact on people."

The words started him thinking about everything. He observed that he had some superciliousness due to his higher education, modernity, and a little progress. On the other hand, the man in front of him was calm and composed. He wore a traditional white kurta, had a white beard and a sandalwood *tilak* on his forehead.

The man went on, "Don't be prejudiced by someone's way of dressing. You never know what they have for you."

It was a savage blow to his initial arrogance. Kumar realized he was right. This was the first time in life he had found himself guilty of arrogance and rudeness.

The man continued, "Let's talk about something that might sabotage your entire aspiration of being successful. There is something that sneaks into you and ruins your mind like a termite."

"Please tell me," was Kumar's only response.

"If you wish to become an impactful speaker, make sure you don't reflect the biggest killer of greatness-superciliousness."

His words were a clear message. He appeared to know exactly what to say. He continued, knowing that Kumar was listening eagerly, "Believe me there is no bigger killer of aspirations than this. No one can stand before it. Let's talk about it."

At Kumar's nod, he went on, "Although it may not harm you directly, it will definitely affect you indirectly and slowly. It eats up your whole enthusiasm and creativity. Eventually it becomes a habit to show off. This tendency turns you into someone who doesn't believe in satisfying himself but the others. Your perspective changes from being a performer to an appreciation-seeker. Eventually your performance loses quality and you lose appreciation too."

"How would one come to know if they have this?" came the natural question.

"Easy. Jealousy and prejudice, frequently giving expert advice to others."

He went on to explain the following signals to know if you have those traits:

- Jealousy:

    - You become uneasy when someone boasts about themselves or someone is appreciated before you. It doesn't matter if that person is your friend or your enemy.

    - You may not express it, feel it inside. Observe yourself and stay honest to yourself.

    - Instead of appreciating you start criticizing others more. Check how many times you appreciate or criticize people in a day. The former must be several times more than latter in order to have a healthy psyche and positive energy.

- Frequent Expert Advice:

    - You offer unasked suggestions

    - You dominate a discussion, without listening to contrary points

    - You expect your advice to be followed and if not, it hurts your pride.

- You listen less and react more to people and situations. It results in weakening your inner strength and mental balance which makes you vulnerable and less smart.

- Prejudice:

  You carry a sense of superiority because of your background or success or something and you think others opinions as unimportant or unworthy. You don't talk to new people much. Before talking, you create preconceived notions based on their appearance or other attributes, like you did with me."

Don't be in a hurry to be a good speaker. Be a good listener." With those words he got up and deboarded the train.

Chapter: 15

Impact of Listening To A Wise Man

❖ **Conversations With Right People Is Transformational**

When Kumar came back home, he made notes about the journey, especially of what the man had said.

It's imperative to be aware of these negative aspects of yourself. You should be clear on *what you are not* when you aspire to be a super speaker. You must know what crucial you may miss if you have these traits.

His interaction with the old man helped him realize this, something he shared with his trainees.

"Look at yourself as an observer. See if the following happening:

- You still listen to others quite often. Stay honest.

- Your reaction to people disagreeing or criticizing you. Is it strong or humble?

- Your loved ones and well-wishers are happy with you. If not, make sure they are.

"Despite your observations, it might come in at any stage of progress. It's more inconspicuous and insidious than the best predator. Make a habit of asking yourself these questions regularly and update your observation. The same way you update your computer software. This way you can defend yourself against supercilious virus."

He wrote "Your progress is not contradictory to others happiness. You must remain open to new ideas. You will see that not only you but also the people around are growing."

Secondly, he once again wondered about the beauty of asking right questions (to oneself).

"How well these questions could guide you" He smiled thinking about the new questions he got after meeting the old wise man.

The visit to Rishikesh changed Kumar's approach. Now he wanted his journey to benefit as many people as possible. Earlier, it was more about his own progress and fulfilment of his dreams but now he had understood that a great responsible person should think for the benefit of others. As a speaker and trainer, it's always about your listeners. The old man on the train was right. The path to staying longer started from how well you benefit others.

Kumar made this lesson a mantra. He decided to share this with all his trainees.

"Call it GFS," announced Kumar in his training session. "It's like the GPS system in cars that guide us on our journeys, we need to install this GFS in our heart to help ourselves. The GFS stands for

- Genuineness

- Fearlessness

- Steadfastness

"How can one develop these qualities?" asked a trainee.

"It's not that we don't have these qualities, everyone is born them. However, depending on your upbringing, experiences and personal inclinations, some qualities rise to the surface while others are buried. The former gets polished, the latter fade." Kumar explained.

"Does that mean, once faded it disappears?" asked someone.

"Not actually. Any quality is polished through experience, experience where a quality is needed. For example, suppose someone is jittery by nature, can't fight anyone. The same person can fight fiercely if a family member is attacked by someone. He would find courage inside because he needed it at that point of time."

"What about someone who doesn't get enough experience to obtain all the qualities? After all experience is a matter of luck. So, should that person call himself unlucky, because he couldn't gain experience?"

"Well I have a different view. We come across all kinds of situations, however, our preferences and choices decide which situation to face. Accordingly, certain qualities become prominent and others diminish." He responded.

After a little thought, Kumar said, "Let's take an example. Earlier, I used to stay in my comfort zone, I avoided difficult situations. However, I also had the dream of a grand life and speaking on stage. So, mere thought about reaching those kinds of heights didn't get me the essential difficult experiences, to learn the required skills. As a result of the lack of those experiences, qualities like courage to face audience, skills to handle crowds and composure for planning the events etc. never came to me. When I decided to change the course of my life, I started facing those challenges and over time, I realized, I became more comfortable facing of challenges, and new qualities started developing."

"It's more about what you face, based on your own preferences, making our personality." One trainee exclaimed.

"That's the reason, you need to think big, have a big dream. Not just that, you need to have a plan to realize that dream and then take the steps to succeed. That way each day becomes an experience enriching your life."

Another way to look at it is:

If a person doesn't gain enough experience because he

stayed in his comfort zone, what does he need in order to install GFS to realize his dreams?

"The answer is simply earning experience. If you know that you haven't got those experiences, you must decide to get them now. Find ways to create those experiences. Put yourself into situations where you need those qualities.

Let's go back to the earlier example, suppose an armed intruder, a thief, has barges into your home and points a gun at one of your family members.

Now you are an ordinary person who's never fought anyone. And the situation before you, tells you that your family members are in danger. Your mind forces you to do something. Several ideas bombard your mind, multiple options running through it. You know you must show courage before it gets too late while another part of you pushes for caution. Your mind is struggling with the most suitable options and the timing.

Now think of the situation you are in. Think of the qualities you have currently.

- Your courage is soaring

- You have unprecedented commitment towards saving the person

- You are creatively thinking of new ideas

- You care like never before

- You are alert

- You can feel how important a life is, just one shot, one split second and the person is dead

- You understand how precious time is, each minute, each second, each millisecond

- You feel the connection of love and family as at that moment you'll sacrifice your life for another's.

- You also realize of the 'law of uncertainty', you know that certain things are always uncertain.

  All the qualities that make someone a superhero have suddenly arisen in you.

You now have your GFS. Weren't all these qualities always inside you? Just waiting to be revealed given the right situation?

That doesn't mean we expect such situations to happen. This means that we open ourselves to facing the situation, to being open when someone needs our help, to help them without hesitation and in return, Nature will show us the qualities we need.

Chapter 16
The World Is My Oyster

Addressing a crowd of students from a stage wasn't just an aim, but a life-experience Kumar wanted. When he finally thought he was ready to take the leap, conducted a seminar. He took the zest from all the speakers he'd come across, the reverberation of a standing ovation passing through each cell of his body. The seminars of Mr. Akash Gautam, Mr. Arfeen Khan and Robin Sharma had always left him inspired.

"I must plan for an event. This time, it's going to be me, as an iconic speaker addressing a crowd of hundreds. I've had enough of smaller events, I need to push myself." This thought excited him a lot.

He didn't realize when he started penning it in a notebook, but he did realize later that conducting a seminar, on your own, is nothing less than arranging a big marriage. There were too many factors and calculations involved:

- Arranging a venue keeping in mind the expected number of the people, location and budget.

- The quality of light and sound systems for the location

- The marketing including the designing and printing of pamphlets, banners, hoardings, business cards based on your budget and requirement

- Digital marketing on social media, etc.

Along with all those basics, you also have

- Arrangement of water and snacks for the audience

- Set up at the location

- Finding volunteers to help with different tasks, instructing the volunteers about their specific roles and their requirements and expectations

- A database of the people who attended for future communications and technical support to help saving your notes and content organization.

- A cameraman to take videos and photos

- And lastly some of your best friends for honest feedback and a few critics to know what was lacking.

For his first big event, he decided to start well in advance. He started to plan a month in advance. First finalizing a topic; he wanted it to be within his area of expertise something to fire up the audience because they could relate to it. Finally, he selected one and modified it-**How to kill your fear of English**. The title seemed impressive as it conveyed all that he wanted to help his audience with.

The venue came next; a moderate place with the seating capacity of 200 people. He enlisted all the friends who could volunteer and designed and placed the pamphlets, business cards, banners etc. around the city and figured out digital marketing with some tech support. Arrangements like water, snacks, decoration, audio, and video etc. were left for later.

Along with all this, he worked on his content with a view of leaving an impact in the minds of his audience. He didn't want to restrict it to simply a motivational event. He wanted to make some content to help his audience learn about something that they could use easily in their lives. He wanted his audience leave the hall with some sort of improvement.

He spent a week, developing content for a two-hour session. Then it was time to go for his favourite phase-Practice. He practiced of the content – first in parts and then the whole thing. He videotaped himself to check his body language. He carefully went over the content for grammatical mistake and got feedback from friend about his tone. He created a set up on the terrace of his house to practice – a feat that looked crazy to his neighbours.

In the last week before the big event, the final rehearsals were carried out. His excitement soared. He tried hiding his restlessness, but his facial expressions often gave him away. Long forgotten tendencies of apprehension would pop up unexpectedly. His heart would oscillate between negativity and positivity, but he knew how to deal with it now. The final arrangements were completed a few days before the grand event.

The day finally arrived when he had to prove to himself that all his learning wasn't meaningless.

"Have you gone through everything Kumar? Because it's not easy to learn and practice everything in last few hours?" Kumar's distant friend, one of his foremost critics, asked sarcastically.

"Everything I learnt in life was leading up to today" Kumar responded and continued going over the arrangements.

Kumar reached the venue two hours early. Primarily, because he wanted to get used to moving on a real stage but also, to ensure that technical work was good. He wanted to know how loud he had to speak using a collar-mic, it being his first time. The other arrangements were handled by the volunteers.

Being his first big seminar, he had invited all his family members, extended family members and some childhood friends too. He made sure that they sat in the front row to help motivate him.

"Just 10 minutes to go. There're more than 150 people already in the hall and more are still coming. Great job." Dinesh, a friend told Kumar.

"The real picture is yet to come. It's going to be 200 plus. I'm sure about it." Sumit commented.

"Now the rest depends on you Kumar. History is going to be written, write it in golden words" Brahmjeet exclaimed in excitement. But his words had a contradictory effect, it gave him jitters. Kumar was suddenly too nervous to do anything.

Sumit shook vigorously me to wake me up from my panicky daze.

"Oh, um, I was kind of lost. It's going to be difficult." Kumar's discouraging words saddened his friends.

After a minute of silence Brahmjeet decided to say something. "Kumar, you only have 5 minutes to go. Look at your mom in the front row. Look at how proud she is!"

Kumar looked at his mom, who looked back at him. She sent him a thumbs up with a confident smile. Her face showed her pride; after all, this crowd had gathered to listen to her son. Her Kumar was going to be a public figure, going to realize his childhood dream. What else could a mother be proud of?

Then he looked at the person sitting next to her, his elder brother, a father figure to Kumar, who had always been a source of energy for him. He was the one he adored the most. Today, he was also looking back at him with pride and higher expectations of performing, something, which cannot be denied.

"It's a responsibility I had to dispense. I owe this to my family." He thought firmly.

This thought lifted his state of mind instantaneously. Energy erupted within him at the thought of making his family feel proud. He couldn't lose this opportunity.

He took no time in declaring, "It's time to disburse guys, let the magic begin."

He strode to the stage climbed four stairs in two leaps and walked confidently onto centre-stage. His voice rang out as he wished everyone and the audience reciprocated his high energy.

The next 2 hours flew by fast. Kumar enjoyed the session thoroughly. There was no apprehension, no fear, and no hesitation throughout it.

It wasn't that he didn't make mistakes during the seminar. He did, but he was calm and skilled enough now to keep them from affecting his performance. He was able to cover all the topics he wanted to and carried out all activities he had planned. The sustained presence of the audience throughout the seminar also told to his success.

Both the speaker as well as the audience didn't feel like stopping, even at the end. He expressed his gratitude to everyone present; the audience, the volunteers, his friends, cameraman etc. He also wanted the audience to clap for all of these. Then Kumar's clapping for the audience in the end won everyone's heart.

The standing ovation at the end was evident of his glorious effort towards achieving his dream-a dream to be a powerful communicator, a dream to empower people by helping them overcome their weakness, a dream to kill people's fear of English.

After calling it a day and thanking the audience for their wonderful listening skills, the audience disbursed. His friends waited eagerly for him, his family members too. They all were eager to give him a tight hug.

When no one saw any sign of Kumar everyone got curious. No one had a clue about his whereabouts. They looked around to find him but to no avail. Then one of his friends, got on the stage to find a possible trace. There was a small room with curtains on the small entrance on one side of the stage, which was hidden from the front. He curiously stepped towards the room only to find Kumar inside this dimly lit room.

"What are you doing here?" He asked him, puzzled to see him sitting in a meditative pose.

"Nothing." Kumar responded as he wiped his tears. He

smiled looking at the glinting eyes of a performer and stretched his arms for a congratulatory hug.

"It's just the beginning. Reserve these tears for your future performances."

"I'm not going to shed them every time, idiot." Kumar answered, walking onto the stage with his friend and picked up the mic to say something.

"All of you are requested to stay back for a party right here." Kumar's announcement surprised everyone present and by the time, only his family and friends were left. His friends ran up the stage to bring him down amongst everyone. Kumar nudged one of his friends to bring the cake he'd already brought, anticipating this situation, along with the snacks and cold drinks.

The dawn in life, which started from his awareness of his own mediocrity, shortcomings and excuses followed by a right plan and consistent efforts, had grown into a bright beautiful morning. For him, shedding tears of happiness was a unique joy. For years, he had lived a life of excuses that resulted in all his shortcomings, fears, and overall ineffectiveness. There was a time when he even stopped expecting that he would ever do great things in life. Fearful mind, guilt and mediocrity had slowly become kind of integral part of his existence.

But this Kumar was a new one. It was not that he was now sans all shortcomings and fears, but he was undeterred by them because he was also aware of his strengths. He also knew how to make a proper plan and execute it untiringly. He also knew how to move enthusiastically towards his targets.

Now, he was the one who knew how to design his destiny. He was also confident that if he could reach this level from an initial low level, anyone can.

"I can make thousands of students and professionals confident by helping them work systematically on certain things." This thought thrilled him.

Until now, it was more about his own dream of achieving something. But helping others realize their dreams took his spirit to heights.

"I need another comprehensive planning for this ambition." He thought knowing that he could make it.

Chapter 17

Your Greatest Self

❖ **Your Biggest Project Is You**

Kumar got giddy for a moment, imagining himself as a Speaker and Coach. He knew that his journey so far was full of upheavals. From being miserably shy during initial years of his professional life to working tirelessly for IIMs to going reclusive after separating from his beloved and quitting MBA to living uneventful life for years to becoming aware of his childhood dream and reaching where he was now. The whole journey looked fascinating in hindsight. He remembered the days when he was very happy and thought of the reasons behind that happiness.

He remembered that every time he set a difficult target and accomplished that with right planning and tireless efforts, he was filled with great satisfaction and sustained happiness; the effort in

- Preparing for CAT day in and day out

- Working on English and Spoken skills throughout the months and years

- Tasks like 'Super 50 days challenge'

- Now recently, working meticulously for his first seminar

He once again took his favourite diary and noted, **"It's doing the things that bring up your fears and challenge you, ensure you growth and lasting happiness."**

"This means your next project on your health, knowledge, social service or professional life should be more challenging than the previous one" This thought gave him goose bumps.

"What it could be?" He wondered.

Obviously, it would be related to his new-found passion, his self-given title of 'Speaker and Coach'.

His thoughts channelized him backward to the point he started from- why did I want this?

It took him to the original purpose- to influence people.

Since then, he had travelled a long way and had seen various stages. He had also grown mature now and grown out of the initial excitements from superficial praise and standing ovations. Now, he wanted something of pure substance. Something that changed the lives of people, along with happiness for him.

"Influence people to transform their life" The idea was thrilling.

He started making plans about his new journey as a speaker and coach with this new clarity and greater purpose. He remembered clearly that his aim was primarily to help people realize their dream of becoming a powerful speaker. He also knew that plans work well only when a clear target is given. **Vague goals hardly result into something important**.

He thought something and noted down in his diary in bold letters, **"6 months, 100 people; 6 months 10 people"**

He gave himself a target that in next 6 months, he would help 100 people kill their fear of English. He took this as a mission for next half a year. The reason behind choosing this was that he believed that rest of all professional achievement would follow effortlessly, if this barrier was broken.

Simultaneously, he put another goal of helping 10 people get a job by helping them with their interview preparation within the same period.

He knew the power of words and right way to communicate. Powerful communication would help them perform well in interviews and presentations, strengthen their relationships and friendships, positively influence people during conversations and create an overall positive energy around themselves.

So, he thought of designing his program in a way that could help these many people first face this fear and then under his guidance overcome it systematically.

He knew that motivation only helps one percent, the rest is all effort under right process. He had to include a blend of motivation and systematic process to make people achieve actual results.

Sitting in his study, he noted down in his diary, "This journey is quite unique and appears to be both challenging and exciting."

He realized that challenge and excitement are two faces of the same coin. He was at an uplifted state of mind where nothing seemed daunting. However, he wanted to plan out his program in a way that results him into maximum.

He decided to execute his plan by launching a meeting spree with the students and professionals using digital platforms. He also went for free seminars in colleges and universities where he could find those students in plenty who were willing to get helped.

Thereon, he embarks on a new exciting journey. After various interactions, he made the first batch of 20 selective people with whom he would work intensively for next few weeks, an exclusive club of members who he called as 'Performers'.

He used his techniques mixed with motivation and worked persistently. He clearly told his performers that success didn't come through shortcuts, instead with clarity of goal, sticking to your plan and moving enthusiastically.

He introduced best of his learnings like setting up a target like

> ➢ 'Super 50 days' to gain momentum and achieve greater degree of commitment

> ➢ Face your fears to conquer your fears

> ➢ 5-step system to attain your goal

Soon, his training paid off.

He could see a clear improvement among his trainees in the form of

- **Higher confidence**

- **Deeper belief in their goals**

- **Greater momentum**

Then came more tangible results when they started showing magical results in different areas of their lives, especially their professional lives.

Some even reported that their relationship status had improved and they had minimal clashes with their loved ones.

Most of them said that people paid more attention to what they said during casual meetings.

Almost all of them, reported that their language had become less wordy and pithier. This made their self-confidence soar.

With all this feedback, Kumar knew that this was what he wanted and the rest of success in life would naturally come to them.

Happy with the success stories of his trainees, he carried out another meeting spree with students from different colleges, this time more specifically he chose MBA students who were struggling with their communication skills and hesitant to face interviews. Finally, he completed the batch of 20 people for this month and next 20 for next month.

This time he gave them a target of 50 days only as per his 'Super 50 days' methodology, knowing that the confidence they wanted to gain could be easily increased manifold within short time under a right process.

Four dream months passed and he was enthusiastically nearing his target of '100 people and 10 people'.

He formed a last batch of 20 people to complete the target. The practice was going at the right pace when, after 15 days of practice, 3 trainees approached him.

"Kumar, we want to become influential communicators and want to become a speaker. Please help." One trainee requested on behalf of all three.

These words thrilled Kumar as this is the first time he had come across with a trainee with a similar inclination as his.

"Definitely. But why do you want to become a speaker? Tell me one by one."

Kumar had to be sure of their purpose before offering any help. He knew that sometimes people just casually ask for things, even when they haven't put serious thought behind it.

"It fascinates me the way you speak on stage and impact others. I want to speak like that too. It's challenging, but now I believe more in myself." One of them spoke clearly.

"I'm not sure, but I've observed that I've improved on my communication skills. And I don't want to restrict myself to the traditional field of Engineering. I know my communication skills will get me a good job now, but I also know that they can take me to greater heights too. May be that's why." Second trainee gave an elaborate convincing answer.

"I found it a good way of earning name and fame and also an excellent way of social service when you uplift people psychologically." Came the honest reply from the third.

Kumar was astonished with these replies. All these were same as what he had initially. His eyes gleamed after knowing their purposes, and partially because, his training was showing the results he was looking for.

He wanted people to gain confidence and look beyond their present capacity and aim for it.

"Kumar, we want it as soon as possible. Tell us, how soon can we become a speaker? It's too difficult to hold the excitement. If you suggest, we can organise an event tomorrow." Said the three enthusiastically.

Kumar wholeheartedly offered his support to them, he also ensured them that they would realize their dreams very soon. Along with this, he also gave them a caveat that he had to stay committed toit and it was not wise to go out unprepared and unplanned and regret later. **"For an ordinary goal, you make ordinary efforts. For extraordinary goals, you need extraordinary efforts."**

But before we start, let me tell you a story of 'Three lions'.

He started telling the story as the three trainees sat in front of him:

"There were 3 lions in a zoo. They were all healthy and extremely proud of themselves as every visitor called them 'King of the Jungle' or 'Mighty Beast' etc. They'd always dreamt of living a free life in the jungle. For a long time, they demanded their release. They'd heard that the natural place for lions is the jungle, not the zoo. Some animal rights activists visited the zoo and heard the lions' demands. They filed a case against the zoo authority and the forest department under which they were kept in the zoo for the lions. After a few days they returned with a court order to set the lions free.

The lions were released but some people advised them to be careful as the jungle was a dangerous place and life wasn't easy there. But the lions didn't heed their advice, too sure in their might. They were taken to a jungle and released, all excited to live their new life in freedom.

After a few days, the same activists and some scientists too became curious if lions had acclimatized to their new environment in the jungle. All expected the lions to be happy living in their natural habitat. So, they went to the jungle and searched but they found no trace of the lions.

Everyone wondered where the lions went. The forest authority assured everyone that it was impossible for the lions to leave the jungle as there were fences around the boundary. But no trace could be found. After considering all options and possibilities they decided to carry out another search. This time they were successful in discovering just their skeletons in different areas of the jungle. They were astonished. They discussed the various possibilities behind these mysterious deaths:

The very first possibility they came up with was that the lions were killed by some other lions already living in the jungle. But the forest department dismissed this possibility saying that there were no others in the jungle.

The second possibility was that they were hunted by poachers, a possibility negated by the forest department saying that poachers weren't active in the area. Even if poachers had killed them, they would have taken away their entire bodies, there was no point in leaving the skeletons.

The last possibility was that they might have killed each other out of hunger. But this wasn't possible as their skeletons were in different areas of the jungle. Everyone there was perplexed about what happened to the lions."

He took a pause for a moment.

"Can you think of any clue?" Asked Kumar.

He smiled looking at them as they shook their head clueless and yet curious, expecting him to answer.

"Well. Let me share the startling fact scientists found. Those mighty lions were hunted by the wild dogs."- He grinned, enjoying their wonder.

"Unbelievable! The largest hunters hunted by dogs?!"-

Everyone was obviously baffled, unable to put it together. "How can they have been hunted by dogs?"

"It's a fact you have to believe. The fact is that those zoo lions, had lost their natural instincts, skills and fearlessness while living in the zoo. After their release they were simply as helpless in front of a wild pack of dogs. No Surprise! No astonishment! A simple consequence of living in a protected environment of a zoo."

When I heard this story the first time I was equally surprised. I wrote the following points down in my diary:

1. RIGHT ENVIRONMENT BRINGS OUT THE BEST:

We learn, grow, and win only when we polish ourselves in an environment that supports. Success never comes in a safe, cozy and comfortable environment, like the lions living in the zoo.

I connected it back to my previous points about 'Dark Surroundings.' I found this was the other side of the coin; while dark surrounding was dangerous because it distracted you or made you lazy. This learning here showed the impact of the right environment on your strengths.

2. DARE TO DREAM BUT DARE MORE TO TAKE STEP:

If the most skilled natural predator could lose its skills

and confidence by living in a protected environment, it's certainly possible for human beings to lose theirs while living in such an environment. So, keep polishing your skills and don't let your essential skills rot.

Confidence enables a leap only when you have right skills otherwise it's as risky jumping from a plane without a parachute.

"Success is not all about removing weaknesses, but it's more about polishing your strengths." I remembered reading it from one of my favourite books.

3. FIGHT ONCE YOU ARE WELL EQUIPPED:

It's unwise to confront a deadly risk without the required skills and confidence. It was foolish of the lions to go into a new environment without a plan, the right skills or time to acclimatize.

Kumar took a deep breath after sharing these points down. He made all the three understand how important it was to have right skills, right environment, and planning before going out to chase your dream.

He related this learning with his own chasing of dreams. His dream of becoming a powerful speaker was there to be fulfilled. He thought of going ahead with a good planning alongside learning right skills. For that he needed a right step in that direction. He decided to go ahead with that.

They found this impressive story very meaningful before going on the path to achieving their goals in life.

"Now we get it even more clearly why do you lay so much emphasis on planning and practice."

"Correct. Now let's meet the day after tomorrow."

Their glinting eyes reflected their soaring enthusiasm. Their confident body language showed their unshakable belief in themselves. Their new dreams of becoming a speaker and influence their audience was evidently holding true to the adage; 'like begets like' and 'law of attraction' that you meet like-minded people. This small meaningful meeting with them also made his belief firmer that not only yawns, infections, and sadness, but also positive qualities like smile, confidence, hope, commitment, and dreams are contagious.

Chapter 18

You Are Your Own Super Hero

❖ **A Hero Is The One Who Takes Charge of His Life**

It was evening and the sun hadn't set, he was sitting in his study lost in thought. The petrichor emanating from outside pulled him back to the beautiful reality of the heavy rain outside. He turned off the air conditioning and opened the window to welcome the cool breeze and rain. He couldn't help but stick out his face from the window to feel it on his face.

His mother's call brought him back.

"Your green tea is on the table" said his mother as she left the room.

He contemplated everything while he drank his tea and the scenery outside.

Kumar was thrilled after interacting with the three trainees yesterday. Their words seemed like the most beautiful words ever spoken.

He wondered why it was so pleasant to hear those words. He'd met so many incredible people, and had liked their words, but there was something special about the interaction with those three yesterday.

"What so special was there in my interaction with them? Why did I like it so much?" He was puzzled.

He closed his eyes again and the whole incident flashed to his mind making him smile. The incident ceased to lose its beauty even after reliving it so many times in mind. It was quite unusual.

In happiness, it was a similar to what a lover feels when his beloved accepts his proposal the first time. In beauty, it was like a sight of peacock dancing in the rain. He took his dairy and started writing.

After writing the whole thing, a realization made him stop writing, and he put down the pen, and looked outside for a moment smiling.

"The most beautiful form of success occurs not when you win, but when you make others win." He put his realization in simple words.

Now he understood why that simple interaction gave him so much happiness. So far, it was only about his goals. All the effort he had made so far were to achieve his personal ambitions. He did achieve them, with the right planning and methodical endeavour. Even training people was a part of his goals. It made him feel proud of himself.

Yesterday, three trainees approached him with their own goals, goals which were similar to his own. Their approaching him was evident of the effectiveness of his program. It meant that he was able to help people go beyond where they currently were, to succeed as he had.

He realized that their higher potential in the future was what made him feel so excited. By thinking of their aptitudes, he was taking vicarious joy. He had orchestrated his destiny, now he had an opportunity to transform theirs. His trainees were going to be great speakers and he was going to help them embark on this scintillating journey to a magnificent future. This image was enthralling.

"Only winners make others win" He stopped with a surprising aspect of this statement.

He thought that he successfully reached at this stage of life where he can help others realize their dreams and become successful. Now others too can reach heights. Taking others there would add greater meaningfulness to his life.

An internet blog also helped him understand the reason behind his deep happiness. He came to know that studies have repeatedly shown the well-being-boosting and depression-lowering benefits of helping others or volunteering. Moreover, there's now neural evidence that suggests a link between generosity and happiness in the brain. For example, donating money for a cause or volunteering during a tragedy, activates the same regions of the brain that respond to monetary rewards or physical pleasures. In fact, the mere intent and commitment to generosity can stimulate neural change and make people happier.

This may be the reason why he found immense happiness from the words of his trainees. Their words were an evidence of the effectiveness of his training. Secondly, the prospect of mentoring them to catapult them to a much higher level in life was perhaps stimulating a neural change that was making him so much happy.

Now this strengthened his commitment to work on their dreams. It was a new exciting challenge. But he knew what he had to do. Three steps:

> a meticulous plan

> a kick start

> a tenacious chase

The next day he handed them over a file titled 'My journey to Speaking Out Fearlessly'. They opened it to see a detailed plan in which they had to fill their details. Like-

a) Recognize your strengths and weaknesses

b) Define your dream precisely and ask the right question of why you want to pursue it

c) Find your Dark areas like

Dark Core

Dark Pathway

Dark Surrounding

Dark Driving

Find how could you brighten these areas

d) Engineer a high energy body

e) Make a plan to work on your fears and all other challenges

   Make a to-do list with precise details of how you're going to work on them

   Make a list of outcomes you want from your plan

f) Kick-start your journey by tenaciously working for 'Super 50 Days'

g) Unleash your greatest self by

   - Improvising your plan if needed

   - Expanding your dimensions by giving yourself bigger challenges

   - Calibrating your language and words to speak powerfully

"Kindly fill in the details honestly and without hesitation. Take your time. We're going to start this exciting journey tomorrow onwards. I'll help you out with point 'd' and 'e'. Once you start you can't back off under any circumstance. Are you with me?" Kumar announced in a stentorian voice to synergize the trainees' excitement.

"Undoubtedly" Trainees chorused.

50 days passed in a jiffy. Each day witnessed greater momentum as they slowly moved ahead initially with some hesitation to later much confidently in face of different challenges. They worked on their hesitation, fears, and barriers and on language and right words. After successfully completing first 4 weeks, they found their confidence soaring.

They wanted to finish their 'Super 50 Days' with a bang. They decided to go for a more difficult challenge to become a speaker. They organized seminars and participated as a speaker. They did a fantastic job and received appreciation.

Kumar was waiting for them in evening at a restaurant as this dinner was on him today. He had promised his trainees to throw a party after their first seminar.

"Now I believe that most of my fears were unfounded. Like yesterday, I addressed a group of people in a market and asked them to join me in singing a song. Some even danced with me!" Said a trainee excitedly as soon as they took seats and started discussion.

"Yes, now I regret that we should have tried to get a bigger crowd like 200 or more." another trainee added giggling.

"Correct. All fears are the product of our mind. Fears

reside within this small sphere called head. It's a muck that we're used to seeing and it's a responsibility to clean up this area to see the real world." said Kumar. **"We can't see the world in its full glory and beauty through the prism of our fear. That's why a fearful mind can't be optimistic, farsighted, or visionary; only a fearless or liberated mind can."** He completed.

"Yes, that's why today we can see our future far more clearly than we could earlier" said one trainee. Two others agreed promptly.

Kumar was wondering about the similarity of experiences which his trainees had had since the time they came to him. Everything from the beginning till today had so much analogous. Their hesitations and desire, and dreams and inhibitions, tenacity and focus, everything seemed so similar. It appeared to him as repetition of his own life in a quick rewind something that made him smile widely in deep satisfaction.

"A dream, seen long ago but kept secretly fuming in the subconscious, later identified, and finally made true."

Now, what are your answers to the questions asked at the beginning of the book:

1. Is each passing year adding more tensions, more frustration, more inactivity, increased illnesses, less smiles per hour in your life?

    Please make a list of what you're losing and What you're gaining every year.

    ____

    ____

2. Do you have a dream?

    If yes, please write it down in most precise words.

    ____

    ____

3. Do you have the courage to fulfil your dream and be the architect of your own destiny?

    If yes, make a plan.

    ____

    ____